T4-BBL-072

For the Love of Reading

For the Love of Reading

Guide to K–8 Reading Promotions

Nancy L. Baumann

Foreword by Richard Allington

LIBRARIES UNLIMITED

AN IMPRINT OF ABC-CLIO, LLC
Santa Barbara, California • Denver, Colorado • Oxford, England

Copyright 2013 by ABC-CLIO, LLC

All rights reserved. No part of this publication may be reproduced, stored in a retrieval system, or transmitted, in any form or by any means, electronic, mechanical, photocopying, recording, or otherwise, except for the inclusion of brief quotations in a review, without prior permission in writing from the publisher.

Library of Congress Cataloging-in-Publication Data

Baumann, Nancy L.
  For the love of reading : guide to K-8 reading promotions / Nancy L. Baumann.
    pages cm
  Includes index.
  ISBN 978-1-61069-189-5 (pbk.) — ISBN 978-1-61069-190-1 (ebook) 1. Reading (Elementary)—United States.
2. Reading (Middle school)—United States. 3. Reading promotion—United States.
4. Children—Books and reading—United States. I. Title.
  LB1573.B3725 2013
  372.40973—dc23   2013025863

ISBN: 978-1-61069-189-5
EISBN: 978-1-61069-190-1

17 16 15 14   2 3 4 5

This book is also available on the World Wide Web as an eBook.
Visit www.abc-clio.com for details.

Libraries Unlimited
An Imprint of ABC-CLIO, LLC

ABC-CLIO, LLC
130 Cremona Drive, P.O. Box 1911
Santa Barbara, California 93116-1911

This book is printed on acid-free paper ∞

Manufactured in the United States of America

Dedicated to the students, educators, parents, and caregivers who enthusiastically participated in all the programs presented in this book.

And to Jim, my biggest cheerleader!

Contents

Foreword

Richard L. Allington, PhD
University of Tennessee

I am pleased to introduce you to Nancy Baumann's book, *For the Love of Reading*. This is a practical book, a very practical book. It is also a one-of-kind book, a "how-to" manual for educators. The book is written from Nancy's perspective as an experienced school librarian. The primary focus of *For the Love of Reading* is a set of strategies for enticing children to read—to read a lot!

This book could not have arrived at a better time. The recent report from the National Endowment for the Arts (2007) that notes that the reading activity of young adults has been dropping since 1980 with four of five 17-year-olds reporting that they read no books for pleasure in the previous year! That is double the number reporting no pleasure reading two decades ago. Today, teens read less than any other age group. That does not mean all is well with older readers since roughly half of the young adults ages 18–24 reported reading no books for pleasure in the past year.

The report notes that as reading activity declines so too does reading achievement. It notes that reading activity decreased among college graduates as well as among other less well-educated citizens. It seems our society and our schools are creating greater numbers of alliterates while reducing the numbers of illiterates. Still, of what use is literacy if there is so much evidence that most literate adults fail to ever much use the literacy proficiencies they have?

As I visit schools across the nation, I am too frequently surprised to find that schools today have no school librarian. Too often paraprofessionals or parent volunteers staff the school library. At one school I visited this past year, the school library was open only before and after school and was staffed by paraprofessionals. The budget for new book purchases the previous year had been $700.00. At other schools I visited, there was no longer any functioning school library.

On top of this, I find there are more classrooms today without any functioning classroom library collection of books that kids might elect to read. As I write this, schools across the nation are spending billions of dollars to upgrade their computer systems so that their students will be able to be tested on the new Common Core State Standards (CCSS). Billions for technology and nothing for the books that kids will need to read to produce any competent performance on those CCSS tests!

Quoting from the National Endowment for the Arts (2007) report:

> The habit of daily reading . . . overwhelmingly correlates with better reading skills and higher academic achievement. On the other hand, poor reading skills correlate with lower levels of financial and job success. At the risk of being criticized by social scientists, I suggest that since all the data demonstrate consistent and mostly linear relationships between reading and these positive results—and between poor reading and negative results—reading has played a decisive factor. Whether or not people read, and indeed how much and how often they read, affects their lives in crucial ways. (pp. 5, 6)

Voluntary reading begins to decline after fourth grade, and the decreases observed suggest an even steeper decline today than was observed 20 years ago. It may be that "readicide," as named by Kelly Gallagher (2009), is at work here. Or, as he notes, far too many schools have removed reading from the school day in an attempt to raise reading scores!

Rather than removing reading from the school day, educators should be looking for ways to increase the amount of reading students do during the school day and developing plans for enticing students to read voluntarily outside of school as well. It is both of these factors that *For the Love of Reading* addresses with an array of school-wide activities.

Each activity presented is designed to stimulate reading activity. Each activity is fully described with a month-by-month and week-by-week plan for implementing and managing the activity. There are essential websites and articles that one might read to develop greater expertise with the activities. All in all, this small book will be a godsend for principals, teachers, and librarians.

It is my hope that as you read this book and select an activity to implement, you will see improvements in the numbers of students who are reading during the school day and reading voluntarily outside of school. Active, engaged readers should be the product our schools are most proud of. But until everyone pays greater attention to whether our students are actually reading, we may be poisoning the well that leads to enhanced success as citizens.

References

Gallagher, K. *Readicide: How Schools Are Killing Reading and What You Can Do About It.* Portland, ME: Stenhouse, 2009.

National Endowment for the Arts. *To Read or Not to Read: A Question of National Consequence.* Washington, DC: Office of Research and Analysis, 2007.

Introduction

Keep doing reading clubs!
Give kids a reason to read.
Make reading fun not boring.
Have fun with the kids.
Have older students read to kindergarteners.

–Emily, 5th grade

Teachers want independent reading time for students to practice skills taught in the classroom, but do not have time in their daily schedule. Kindergarten teachers want students to build vocabulary and basic knowledge, be familiar with well-known picture books and characters, and build a regular family reading time. School librarians want to promote the library, collaborate with teachers, and assist students in building a regular reading habit. Parents and caregivers want to help their children achieve in school and enjoy learning. Lastly, administrators want higher test scores, a school where learning is enjoyed, high morale, family involvement, and, of course, a quiet cafeteria. Reading promotional programming presents reading as an enjoyable activity and does not provide extrinsic rewards. Reading promotional programs align with American Association of School Librarians (AASL) standards and Common Core State Standards by promoting reading as an enjoyable activity and building vocabulary and knowledge from a variety of print and digital materials.

Reading Aloud to Children Is Important

Reading aloud is the number one activity families can do to help their children succeed in reading and school. In addition, it is never too late to begin (Trelease, 2006; Hall and Moats, 2000; Krashen, 2004). Being read to assists children develop vocabulary and hear more rare words than in daily conversation and television scripts. Rare words are those words children need to develop strong vocabularies. Being read to gives children knowledge about the world they live in and interests they have (Trelease, 2006). Children learn word patterns and other essential skills needed for learning to read. Children learn about storytelling, characters, plot, setting, and other literary skills from being read to. Last of all, being read to allows children to share a pleasant experience while learning how to handle a book and discuss a story and illustrations (Hall and Moats, 2000).

Family Involvement

Involving families is one of the strongest factors of a child's success in school regardless of family income or education level. Low-income and racially diverse families are positively affected by being included in ways they can help their child learn. Schools that reach out to parents and caregivers find higher student success than schools that do not enlist parents in the learning process. Higher teacher morale and school satisfaction is also linked to parent involvement. Parents and caregivers who participate as team members to educate their child improve student learning, attitudes about school, and feel greater self-confidence ("Family-School Partnerships," 2000). Schools must recognize the strong component of parent and caregiver involvement and create programs to promote it. Workshops involving families are an excellent way to share information on techniques to work with their child, volunteer opportunities, and community resources (Lautenschlager and Hertz, 1984). Workshops are an informative yet informal setting for families to interact with teachers and other school personnel. Lastly, reading aloud to boys is very important. Boys, especially boys of color, define most of the population in special education, remedial reading classes, and prison. Involving parents and caregivers, older brothers, mentors, and church members in literacy activities for young boys is an important way to support and nurture beginning readers and alliterate readers (Zambo and Brozo, 2009).

Establishing a family reading habit makes television viewing and electronic media less important (Neuman, 1995). Studies show that families who establish regular reading sessions either themselves or through a school program skip television viewing in favor of reading together. Reading aloud is a highly anticipated time for a family member and child to spend together. In addition, reading aloud builds attention span and focus. Listening to a story unfold, finding details in illustrations that enhance a story, and following the words being read require focus, attention, and being able to sit through a book. These skills assist a young child in becoming a successful learner (Zambo and Brozo, 2009). Excessive and especially unsupervised television viewing occurs more frequently for boys in poverty. Hearing a large amount of television language that is spoken at a rapid rate and without any interaction with the viewer is detrimental for essential vocabulary development. Not only are children missing out on normal conversation with an adult, but are also missing out on acquiring the rare words found in books. Watching a lot of television, not being read to, and lack of reading materials is extremely risky for all children but especially those who are at-risk (Trelease, 2006). It is the perfect storm for creating a struggling reader.

Continuing to read to children even though they can read themselves is just as important as reading to young children. Children must constantly build vocabulary and increase their knowledge base. Reading aloud also promotes books and print to children. Readers can listen to books read to them at a higher level than they can read themselves. Numerous studies concur that reading aloud for children of all ages is the best thing a parent, caregiver, or educator can do to promote reading success (Trelease, 2006; Krashen, 2004; Anderson, 1985; Fox, 2008; Hall and Moats, 2000; Zambo and Brozo, 2009). Teachers and parents reading books aloud regardless of age can increase comprehension, listening skills, reading enjoyment, and an exposure to a range of genres and reading materials. Every time a book is read aloud to a child, it sends a message that this book is special and exciting, whereas a worksheet is uninviting. Children look elsewhere for enjoyable activities if no one promotes reading as pleasurable (Trelease, 2006). When surveyed about being read to in class, middle-school students report that besides having independent reading time, they enjoy having their teacher read aloud to them. Teachers that take time to discover high-interest reading for tweens and teens and read dramatically receive high marks. Students feel respected by the teacher who carefully selects a variety of books and reading materials especially for them (Ivey and Broaddus, 2001; Worthy, 2002; Lee, 2011; Blessing, 2005). Read-alouds afford struggling older readers an opportunity to enjoy books at their interest level read fluently beside their peers. Read-alouds build vocabulary, comprehension, and writing skills of older students (Trelease, 2006; Krashen, 2004). Numerous testimonies from students, teachers, and librarians demonstrate change in attitudes and motivation through reading to older students (Trelease, 2006; Worthy, 2002; Krashen, 2006; Blessing, 2005; Ivey and Broaddus, 2001; Lee, 2011).

Reading aloud is beneficial and free. Parents and caregivers must collaborate with school to reinforce skills taught in classrooms. They can improve their child's attention span, vocabulary, knowledge, and reading skill. Families can feel a partnership while working in tandem with the school in their child's education. Teachers, the librarian, school administrators, and parents working together make reading meaningful and fun.

Sustained Silent Reading Time Is Important

Providing consistent time to self-select reading materials and read independently is successful in motivating and engaging students to read. Results from studies demonstrate that while students may not make great gains in their reading skill, they don't lose ground either while participating in a sustained silent reading (SSR) program. Practicing reading through SSR is a necessary component of a successful literacy program (Allington, 2012). However, disagreement between researchers and the NRP panel whether SSR is beneficial is well documented. But a study shows that NRP's findings and those of NRP's lack of data about SSR, lack of agreement among panel members about how research was conducted and explained, the abundance of supporting research in favor of SSR, and preceding studies taking place after the NRP report *favor* the use of SSR in schools (Garan and DeVoogd, 2008; Krashen, 2006).

Using SSR to provide uninterrupted independent reading time gives children a chance to practice reading skills taught in the classroom. Worksheets are not part of SSR. Self-selection of materials is of high interest to students. After all, reading for enjoyment is part of the reason for teaching reading in addition to acquiring knowledge. SSR encourages students to enjoy reading and in the process assists them in building a wealth of background knowledge and vocabulary while improving reading speed and comprehension.

SSR increases motivation, engagement, and positive attitudes toward libraries and reading. Participating in SSR assists younger students by providing time to practice reading skills taught in the classroom while improving attitudes about reading. Students are able to spend time reading without interruption and worksheets. The daily practice allows students to increase the amount of words read as they become more proficient. Students find themselves being able to complete longer books when they are given time to read independently. In addition, students are coming in contact with more "rare" words through reading which in turn expands vocabulary.

Becoming a proficient reader opens doors for everyone. It is a predictor of graduating from high school, pursuing higher education, landing a satisfying job, and becoming a productive member of the community (Krashen, 2006; Zambo and Brozo,2009; Hernandez, 2012). A recent study on struggling readers and high-school dropouts reveals that students not able to read on grade level by third grade are four times less likely to graduate from high school by age 19 than those children who can read proficiently as third graders. If the child is living in poverty, that statistic climbs to 13 times less likely to graduate than an affluent child who is reading proficiently. However, a child in poverty being able to read proficiently can achieve above the 90-percent graduation rate—the same as his or her wealthier peers (Hernandez, 2012). Providing strong reading instruction, SSR, and being read to by dedicated educators and families can create proficient readers who graduate from high school regardless of their race or social status.

Additional and Necessary Components of SSR

Providing SSR time is just the beginning. It is not just "take out your books and read" time. Structuring SSR to ensure only reading is taking place is important. Recommendations for successful SSR time come from many studies (Krashen, 2004; Preddy, 2007; Worthy, 2002; Lee, 2011; Cunningham and Stanovich, 2003). Students must gather reading materials, get drinks, and go to the restroom prior to starting SSR. A choice of reading material is highly important. If students finish a book or magazine, they have extras at their place. Self-selection from high-interest print material is also essential (Krashen, 2004; Ivey and Broaddus, 2001; Zambo and Brozo, 2009; Gambrell, 2011; Worthy, 2002). Magazines, graphic novels, comic books, informational books, and the local newspaper are highly recommended. Mysteries, scary titles, and sports books are top requests by students. Rotating the collection so that readers continue to be interested keeps students interested. Providing a comfortable setting is conducive to promoting SSR time. Allowing students to relax with comfortable extras like floor pillows demonstrates that reading is relaxing. Supervising adults should be reading during SSR. Give students a sharing session with one another once a week. It is important for students to learn from one another what to select next. Recommendations on developing successful SSR programs for schools even in low-achieving schools are widely available to assist educators with supportive research on SSR and solid educational rationale for implementing a program (Gambrell, 2011; Worthy, 2002; Preddy, 2007; Trelease, 2006; Pilgreen, 2000).

Scaffolded SSR or ScSR: A Modification

ScSR takes the best of SSR, regularly scheduled silent reading, and adds informal teacher and student conferences; a variety of genres from which students select reading materials; and book log assignments or reading responses (Reutzel, Fawson, and Smith, 2008). A study with third graders comparing

ScSR to guided repeated oral reading finds both approaches promote fluency and comprehension improvement. Researchers report using one or more than one method to give young students fluency practice was seen as desirable for engagement and motivation. However, teachers and students report using only one approach is tiresome.

Motivation and Engagement, Self-Selection, High-Interest Reading Material, and Access to Books

Less than one-third of 13-year-olds read for pleasure, while the percentage of 17-year-olds reading nothing for pleasure doubled in the last 20 years (Biacarosa and Snow, 2006). We have students that can read but simply do not regardless of difficulty (Allington, 2012). This is not acceptable. We must listen to our students. Students say having current reading materials of interest to them; time to read without any "responsibilities" such as journals, book logs or worksheets; and teacher book talks is motivating. Regularly rotating and updating SSR collections is a must for readers to continually discover new materials. Teachers reading aloud from books and materials selected personally for them is also important to students. A successful SSR program relies on the awareness of educators to keep the program fresh, relevant to students, and structured.

Access to up-to-date and high-interest collections is extremely important for the success for SSR and student motivation and engagement. Students must to be able to discover a school library or public library packed with good books and staffed by professional librarians. Building students' interest and then yanking the rug from under them with outdated collections defeats any effort a school is making to build a reading habit. Numerous studies indicate that many inadequate library collections and staff are frequently located in poverty areas (Allington, 2012; Neuman and Celano, 2001; Krashen, 2006; Kozol, 2012; Zambo and Brozo, 2009). Studies also show that with well-stocked library collections, children in poverty make the same gains as in affluent areas. School communities must evaluate their public and school libraries and work toward improving collections and programming for students. Upgraded libraries result in student improvement. Seeking grants and funding from community resources as well as promoting the library's link to literacy are essential parts of librarians' work.

CHAPTER 1

Beary Special
Readers

I think Beary Special Readers is a great program and a very good reminder to parents about the importance of reading with their child and staying involved in learning activities.
—Indian Paintbrush Elementary Parent, Laramie, Wyoming

Before this program we reading sometimes. Now we reading every day. I want to continue grand opportunity to learning more with my daughter.
—Barnett Shoals Elementary Parent, Athens, Georgia

PURPOSE

To build a home-school recreational reading program, improve sight words and vocabulary, and promote distinguished literature for young children.

GOALS

To provide a daily structured reading time for parents, caregivers, and children.

To build a reading habit.

To read 100 books or more to each child during the school year.

To promote early literacy skills.

To involve community volunteers.

MATERIALS

Weekly reading logs

Beary Special Reader buttons

Stickers

Badge-A-Minit button sets and button maker

Cookies and juice boxes (donation)

Implementation of Beary Special Readers

Preparation for Beary Special Readers

The first step is involving families: what their role is in Beary Special Readers (BSR) and why this program is being implemented. Excellent opportunities to explain BSR are at "open house" at the beginning of the school year or at the first parent-teacher conference. A brief and informative slide presentation by the librarian to introduce BSR at open house is essential. Have the reading log and BSR contract available to describe the program and its benefits. A second opportunity to explain BSR is during parent–teacher conferences. Use this time to meet with parents/caregivers individually to explain BSR. Set up a table in the school foyer or kindergarten wing with the slideshow on a laptop. Meet with parents before or after their child's conference to describe their role in BSR.

Reading Logs

Prepare the reading log to go home every Thursday, for example. One side has the weekly recording log, and the reverse contains recommended reading, brief school announcements, and reading tips. Colored copy paper helps families recognize the reading log. The librarian creates the log and places copies in the teachers' mailboxes on Wednesday. Enter the teacher's name in the teacher space prior to copying the logs. Teachers can assist by writing the child's name on the log or have students write their names when they are capable. This is essential when the librarian or volunteers tally the number of books read weekly. Classroom teachers insert the log in the student's weekly folder that contains student work for the week and class newsletter. Families take out the new log and place completed logs in the weekly folder to return to the teacher on

Friday. During the week, families read and record the titles of the books shared with their children. Encourage families to add extra sheets when they fill up the reading log. Reading logs are returned to the library, where the librarian or volunteer enters the number of books read weekly. Place a designated BSR log basket in the library for convenient drop-off. Students can deliver the logs to the library and place them in the BSR basket. Excel and Google Documents are used for record keeping. It is important to monitor students' reading to note if a reminder from the teacher is necessary, if a child needs books for home reading, or if a volunteer reader is needed. Volunteer readers assist in providing reading sessions weekly to ensure all students are being read to and earn reading buttons. Once a student reaches 25 books read for a grading period (typically nine weeks), the reading button is presented to the child and displayed in a prominent place in the classroom. Teachers apply stickers to the reading button for books read over the 25 requested reading. Each sticker represents 5 additional books read over 25 books.

Beary Special Readers
Reading Record

Name _Collin Krueger_ Teacher **Mrs Groshart**

Week of April 2-8 Week 1 of Beary Special Readers IV

Day	Title of Reading Material
Friday 4/2	101 Dalmations Sleeping Beauty
Saturday 4/3	Me on the Map (Collin read) The Easter Egg (Jan Brett)
Sunday 4/4	The Little Mermaid May's Easter Surprise (Collin reading some parts) The Easter Egg (Jan Brett)
Monday 4/5	Snow White & the Seven Dwarfs The Prince & the Pauper
Tuesday 4/6	Sleeping Beauty
Wednesday 4/7	May's Easter Surprise
Thursday 4/8	Hercules

Thank you for reading with your child. Please log in the books you and your child have read.

Janelle L Krueger
Parent/Guardian Signature

An example of a completed log. Note the parent wrote the child was reading by himself.

Beary Special Reader Buttons

Beary Special Reader buttons.

A new BSR button is created for each nine-week session. Badge-a-Minit button maker and software is used to create the design and assemble buttons. Depending upon the number of buttons needed, allow at least three weeks to design and assemble the buttons. With a little instruction, volunteers can assist in assembling buttons. When the nine-week session begins, the buttons will be ready to present to students and display in the classroom.

BSR Reading Ceremony

The BSR reading ceremony is held at the end of each nine-week grading period. Teachers receive a reminder during Week 8 to schedule a date and time for the buttons to be awarded. The reading ceremony can be held in the library, cafeteria, or classroom. Send invitations a week in advance for parents to eat lunch and attend the ceremony. Holding the ceremony in the cafeteria allows parents to watch their child receive his or her button. Ceremonies can take place directly after lunch so parents will be on hand if they eat lunch that day with their child. Students gather with their class to begin the ceremony. The principal or assistant principal calls the student forward, presents each button individually, and shakes the student's hand, while the librarian pins the button on the student. If the ceremony is in the cafeteria, the audience of first graders and other kindergarten classes watch and applaud. Later, back in the classroom, students enjoy special snack of a large sugar cookie and juice box. These are donated by a local supermarket or bakery.

Volunteers

Adult Volunteers

Not all students are read to or return logs. Therefore, it is necessary to have volunteers who read to students. Volunteers generally read to one or two students once a week. Community volunteers can be recruited through the school website, PTA or PTO meetings, and local newspaper. Districts may require volunteers to complete a volunteer packet prior to participating in an activity. Retirees, university students, local businesses, and parents are good sources for volunteers. Additionally, school volunteers—principal, assistant principal, counselors, literacy coaches, paraprofessionals, and school custodians—can assist in reading to students. A volunteer orientation is led by the school librarian to discuss their role with BSR and be assigned to a classroom and students. Tips for sharing books with students as well as a handout, "Why Reading to Children Is Important" by Susan L. Hall and Louisa Moats, *American Educator* (Spring 2000), are given to volunteers. A volunteer folder with student reading logs is kept in a basket along with a second basket of preselected read-alouds. Volunteers select books from the preselected basket to ensure length, high interest, and appropriate level for kindergarten students. The basket contains several classics such as *Caps for Sale*, award titles such as *A Sick Day for Amos McGee*, Caldecott winner, nonfiction from Capstone or Bearport, and newer titles such as Mo Willems's The Pigeon series. Volunteers read three to four titles to student(s) in a session, record the books read on the volunteer/student reading log, and return the folder to the volunteer basket. Volunteers are honored at the PTA volunteer tea at the end of the school year and sent a thank you note with a photograph of them reading to their students.

Student Volunteers

Student volunteers are another excellent source for providing readers for BSR. Include students with special needs and struggling readers to read to kindergarten students. Ask teachers to recommend students. Schedule a callout meeting during lunch time. Interested students can attend a session to learn about BSR and pick up an application. The callout is presented three times, for example, to accommodate the lunch schedule. Allow one week to complete and return the application. A set deadline is listed on the form. Late and incomplete applications may be considered if additional readers are needed in the future. The library committee reviews the applications and selects students. Notify selected students for an orientation meeting during lunch. Students are selected for one semester. At the end of the semester, inquire if students want to continue or take a semester off. Use prior applications and new student applications to select new volunteers. Students can apply anytime and applications remain on file.

Student Orientation

Hold two mandatory orientation sessions in the library during lunch time. Students bring their lunches. The sessions are presented several times to accommodate each lunch period. Orientation includes welcoming students and thanking them for participating as a volunteer. Next, explain the purpose for BSR and their role in providing a reading time for their student listener. Discuss the importance of reading to young children and how it builds beginning reading skills, vocabulary, and a reading habit. Present a skit to demonstrate appropriate reading positions and the importance of expression and comments from the listener. Two students can provide a scenario so that student volunteers understand how to pick up their listener from the classroom, make small talk with them, and lead them to a quiet spot to read. The students select several books from the preselected group of books. After reading, the reader records the books and date on the volunteer reading form and places it in the volunteer reader basket. Last of all, the kindergartner is walked back to his or her classroom. Baskets of preselected books are available for student volunteers. Books are rotated weekly and include a variety of picture books, nonfiction, and magazines. Student volunteers are encouraged to check books out and practice at home. For example, student volunteers can read for 20 minutes before school starts. This is the time when students are in the classroom but school has not begun. Another option for students to be read to is during "quiet time" or "mat time." Discuss the weekly reading schedule and sign-in with student volunteers. Student volunteers read twice a week, Tuesday/Thursday or Monday/Wednesday. They have different students for each session to accommodate the number of volunteers and listeners. Keep track of the number of hours and books student volunteers read each semester. Student volunteers are honored with a luncheon and certificate at the end-of-the-year honors assembly.

Results of the Beary Special Readers Program

This program began in Athens, Georgia, and was also part of library programming in Laramie, Wyoming, and presently in Columbia, Missouri. Each school's kindergarten classes participated. In Athens, prekindergarten and the autistic primary classes joined the kindergarten classes, while in Columbia, first grade and kindergarten classes participate. At the end of the year, parents are invited to provide their comments regarding the BSR program.

BSR Results
+ Each student had a minimum of 25 books per grading period read to him or her and 100 books minimum per school year.

+ Each student received 4 BSR buttons during the year. Many students proudly wore the buttons for several days or placed them on backpacks.

+ One kindergarten class read 1,334 books in a nine-week session. Additional classes averaged about 1,000 books read to students in nine weeks.

+ Parents and caregivers wrote on the reading log that the child insisted on reading to them.

+ Many parents reported that their children are asking to be read to at a specific time.

+ A visiting scholar from Korea reported that the BSR reading helped her and her child become proficient in English.

+ Parents reported that their children are requesting to visit the public library or local bookstore for additional books.

- Several reading grants were received to provide classroom libraries so that students could take home more books to read.

- The number of volunteer readers increased through community and school members.

- The University of Wyoming defensive squad of the football team provided readers twice a week.

- A University of Georgia student changed her major to elementary education/early childhood after volunteering in the BSR program.

Step-by-Step Preparation for BSR

Preplanning—End of the School Year (May or June)

- Meet with the library committee, kindergarten teachers, literacy coach, and principal to plan the implementation of BSR for the beginning of next school year.

- Secure donations of cookies and juice boxes for the four BSR ceremonies.

School District Teacher Preplanning (August)

- Schedule BSR presentation for open house.

- Prepare a brief slide presentation and handouts for families.

- Have the BSR reading information sheet and reading contract available for families.

- Recruit BSR reading volunteers.

- Include a request for reading volunteers in the PTA newsletter and school website.

- Copy BSR reading logs per classroom enrollment. Lightly colored copy paper is an eye-catching reminder.

- Purchase button maker machine, software, and button kits.

- Plan BSR reading volunteer orientation.

First Week of School

- Prepare and copy Reading Log 1 to be delivered to teacher mailboxes on Thursday morning.

- Send an e-mail reminder to participating teachers that BSR Reading Log 1s are in their mailboxes on Thursday morning.

- Request class lists from the office for reading log tally.

- Work with technology coordinator to set up BSR reading log tally on Excel or Google Documents program.

- Contact volunteers and invite them to orientation.

- Make a BSR basket for participating classrooms. Teachers or students place completed logs in the baskets on Friday mornings.

Second Week of School

- E-mail teachers reminders to deliver BSR logs to the library's BSR basket.

- A volunteer or librarian takes the logs and enters the reading log totals.

- Conduct BSR volunteer orientation after school.

- Prepare and copy Reading Log 2 to be placed in mailboxes on Thursday.

Third through Eighth Week of School

- Design BSR buttons using "Badge-A-Minit" software.

- Make 10 extra buttons. A color printer or color copier is needed.

- Hand cut or use the Badge-a-Minit automatic "Cut a Circle" to cut out buttons.

- Assemble buttons. This can be an on-going process until Week 9.

- Place buttons in teacher mailboxes for students who have reached 25 books.

- Put students' names on the back of the button.

- Provide stickers to teachers for additional books read.

- Continue to prepare, deliver, and pick up reading logs.

- Provide a list to teachers of the reading log tally sheet, which can also be accessed on Google Documents.

- Assign adult reading volunteers to students.

- Collaborate with teachers and volunteers for a convenient schedule for the student and the volunteer.

- Have volunteer reading logs and books in baskets for volunteer readers.

Ninth Week of School

- Indicate this is the last week of BSR Session I on Reading Log Week 9.

- Send e-mail to teachers and principal an attachment of the reading totals for the nine weeks.

- ✦ Place BSR buttons in teacher mailboxes so all students have a button.
- ✦ Collaborate with teachers and principal on date, time, and location of BSR ceremony.
- ✦ Remind teachers to invite family members to the ceremony.
- ✦ Check with business on cookie and juice donation.

Tenth Week of School

- ✦ Hold individual BSR ceremonies for all classes.
- ✦ Ask teachers to have buttons ready and placed in a Ziploc bag or basket and brought to the library prior to the ceremony.
- ✦ Take photographs during the ceremony.
- ✦ Write a thank you note and enclose a photograph to the business who donated the snacks.
- ✦ Send a photograph and article about BSR to the local newspaper for the "School News" section.
- ✦ Begin the cycle over again for each nine-week session of the school year.

Don't Forget!!

Beary Special Readers ceremony is on Thursday, October 12, after your class finishes lunch. Please step onto the stage. Have your students' buttons ready (put names on back).

Mr. Clark or Dr. Schmidt will praise and introduce each child. Teachers can assist in pinning on buttons. Invite parents to eat that day with their child and watch the ceremony!! It is fun. Cookies after the ceremony in your classroom.

PreK's ceremony will take place in their respective classrooms with Dr. Schmidt and Mr. Clark as Masters of Ceremonies. Have your buttons ready with names on back.

New 9-week reading period begins Friday, October 6! Happy Reading!

 From *For the Love of Reading: Guide to K–8 Reading Promotions* by Nancy L. Baumann. Santa Barbara, CA: Libraries Unlimited. Copyright © 2013.

Beary Special Readers Volunteer Application

(Open to all 2nd–5th graders)

Beary Special Readers volunteers pick up a kindergarten student on Tuesday/Thursday or Wednesday/Friday and read to that student in the library. Volunteers must be in the library by 7:30 A.M. with their kindergarten listener. Return application by Friday, September 8.

Name	
Grade	
Teacher	
Why do you want to be a Beary Special Readers volunteer?	
Why do you think you will be a good volunteer?	
Favorite author(s)	
Hobbies and interests	
Are you good at working with small children?	
Teacher reference & date	
Parent(s) signature & date	
Student signature & date	

From *For the Love of Reading: Guide to K–8 Reading Promotions* by Nancy L. Baumann. Santa Barbara, CA: Libraries Unlimited. Copyright © 2013.

Beary Special Readers
Week #5

All Day, All Night: A Child's First Book of African American Spirituals—Bryan

Angus Lost—Flack

Chicka Chicka Boom Boom—Martin

Pigs from A to Z—Geisert

Blueberries for Sal—McCloskey

Counting Wildflowers—McMillan

Curious George Rides a Bike—Rey

Horton Hears a Who—Seuss

A Letter to Amy—Keats

Over, Under, and Through—Hoban

Sheep in a Jeep—Shaw

Tar Beach—Ringgold

Abuela—Dorros

Cherries and Cherry Pits—Williams

Feelings—Aliki

Henry and Mudge Take the Big Test—Rylant

Nettie Jo's Friends—McKissack

Noise on Neighborhood Street—Greenfield

The Patchwork Quilt—Flournoy

The Amazing Bone—Steig

Alphabatics—MacDonald

Bigmama's—Crews

Chicken Little—Kellogg

Fish Is Fish—Lionni

Goggles—Keats

The Mitten—Brett

Peter's Chair—Keats

The Napping House—Wood

Strega Nona—de Paola

Uncle Elephant—Lobel

The Black Snowman—Mendez

The Doorbell Rang—Hutchins

Harry, the Dirty Dog—Zion

A New Coat for Anna—Ziefert

Mufaro's Beautiful Daughters—Steptoe

Read before bed. Read after dinner. Read on Saturday evening. Read your favorite story. Read to your child anytime. Your child will appreciate you spending time with him or her. Your child will learn to read with your help. Thank you for reading with your child.

 From *For the Love of Reading: Guide to K–8 Reading Promotions* by Nancy L. Baumann. Santa Barbara, CA: Libraries Unlimited. Copyright © 2013.

Beary Special Readers

Help your child enjoy reading and build a recreational reading habit by reading to your child. Every time you read to your child and record the books you have read together, you help (your school) elementary get closer to its goal—to develop lifelong readers.

Regulations for Becoming a Member of the Beary Special Readers

1. The child will be read to by someone like mom, dad, relative, or caregiver.
2. Books read will be recorded on the **Beary Special Reading Log**. Write down the title of the book(s). Keep the **Reading Log** in a folder, binder, or on the child's bedside table.
3. If the same book is read again, just record it again on the day it was read.
4. Return the completed **Reading Log** on Thursday. Every Thursday, a new **Reading Log** will go home with your child so you can begin reading over the weekend.
5. Both parent and child must sign the contract.

Tips for Sharing Books with Your Child

- Read together daily.
- Set aside a special time and place to read together.
- Discuss the interesting parts of the story with your child.
- Give characters special voices and put in sound effects. It helps your child's listening skills.
- Ask your child to connect with the text by following along from left to right as you read. Point out the pictures and talk about what you see.
- Talk about the story when you finish reading.
- Ask your child open-ended questions, like "What do you think will happen next?" or "What would you do?"
- Read the story over again. Children need to hear favorite stories over and over. It helps them recognize words and remember words. It also helps them predict what is coming next.

Read as many days as you can for as long as your child maintains interest and enthusiasm. Never mind if you skip a day or two. KEEP IT FUN. DO WHATEVER WORKS FOR YOU!

Our goal for Beary Special Readers is for each child to have at least 25 books read to him or her each 9-week grading period.

CONTRACT

I wish to become a lifelong reader and a member of the Beary Special Readers by reading books as often as I am able. I will strive to read at least 25 books every 9 weeks.

_____   _____
(Student's signature)   (Parent's signature)

Beary Special Readers Survey

Parents: Beary Special Readers is a reading incentive program to help your child increase his or her recreational reading and become a reader. Please comment on how you feel about the Beary Special Readers program.

Did you and your child have a regular reading time to read and record books? Please explain.

Did your child ask you to read to him or her? Please comment.

Did your child ask to buy books or go to the library or bookstore for books to read? Please explain.

What kinds of reading material did you and your child read?

Did your child begin to read books to you during the year? Please comment.

Should (your school) elementary continue to have a reading program like Beary Special Readers? Please comment.

 From *For the Love of Reading: Guide to K–8 Reading Promotions* by Nancy L. Baumann. Santa Barbara, CA: Libraries Unlimited. Copyright © 2013.

Beary Special Readers
Reading Record

Name_____   Teacher_____

Week of: (Insert your dates)   **Session:** (Insert your session)

Day	Title of Reading Material
Friday	
Saturday	
Sunday	
Monday	
Tuesday	
Wednesday	
Thursday	

Thank you for reading with your child. Please log in the books you and your child have read.

_____

Parent/Guardian signature

From For the Love of Reading: Guide to K–8 Reading Promotions by Nancy L. Baumann. Santa Barbara, CA: Libraries Unlimited. Copyright © 2013.

Beary Special Readers
Volunteer Reader Schedule

Tuesday/Thursday Readers

Aguilar	Burns	NN	Short	Reagan
Madeline	Kimberly	Anna Grace	Tristan	Markia
Zachary	Chloe	Morgan	Jackie	Jayleen
Christopher P.	Tim Carruth	Aneisha	Courtney D.	Taylor P.
Rameela	David Bell	Tylor P.		

Wednesday/Friday Readers

Aguilar	Burns	NN	Short	Reagan
Jake B.	Khiaiya	Jasmine	May	Lauren
Yuge X.	Caroline	Elizabeth	Lindsey	Sutton
Grace Y.	Guillermo	Seabon	Abigale	Denise
		Braxton		

Volunteers: Please Read This!

- Come to an orientation meeting on Tuesday, October 4, at 7:30 A.M. in the library.

- Check when you are scheduled. Your name is highlighted on the schedule.

- Readers report to the library by 7:30 A.M., sign in, get three appropriate books to read, and pick a place to sit.

- Then you will go to pick up your student and his or her reading log.

- You must eat breakfast before you come to the library.

- After reading and recording, return your books and your student to his or her classroom.

- Questions, see Mrs. Baumann or Mrs. Shaw!

 From *For the Love of Reading: Guide to K–8 Reading Promotions* by Nancy L. Baumann. Santa Barbara, CA: Libraries Unlimited. Copyright © 2013.

You Are Invited!!!

Beary Special Readers Celebration

Where:

When:

Time:

Why: Please join us to celebrate your child's achievement of having 25 or more books read during the past 9 weeks. You may eat lunch with your child and watch the ceremony following lunch.

 **Notes**

CHAPTER 2

Early Bird Readers

I come to Early Bird Readers (EBR) because it gives me a chance to sit back and get lost in a book.

—Harrison, fourth grade

I come to get some reading done and stretch my mind in the morning.

—Christina, fifth grade

PURPOSE

To provide a consistent sustained silent reading (SSR) program for students in order to become proficient readers.

GOALS

To provide a daily structured SSR time for students.

To provide SSR outside of the classroom.

To entice struggling, alliterate, and ESOL students in building a reading habit.

To strengthen vocabulary, fluency, and comprehension.

To demonstrate to students that reading is a pleasurable activity.

To introduce students to a variety of reading materials.

To meet American Association of School Librarians (AASL)/Common Core State Standards of vocabulary acquisition, reading for pleasure, and reading for information.

MATERIALS

EBR sign-in logs and grade-level signs

Large number of graphic novels, high interest fiction and nonfiction at various reading levels, comic books, audiobooks, magazines, and daily newspaper

Tubs or crates for storing books

Raffle slips and containers

Weekly raffle items—school supply items from Geddes, Oriental Trading, Dollar General

Picture frame kits—Geddes or Oriental Trading

ALA READ poster software

Implementation of Early Bird Readers

Preparation for Early Bird Readers

Early Bird Readers (EBR) is a collaborative initiative with the school librarian, classroom teachers, paraprofessionals, literacy and ESOL coaches, administrators, and parents. While the majority of supervision and program management comes from the librarian, others on the EBR team can assist in duties to make the program run smoothly. Teachers and coaches encourage and praise students for attending. Paraprofessionals and parent volunteers assist the librarian with supervision, morning setup and cleanup, record-keeping, and photography. Parents, specifically PTA, and administrators provide funding for raffle items, floor pillow/beanbag chairs, and photography needs. This group should meet at the end of the preceding school year to plan for the implementation of EBR. Additionally, the EBR steering committee meets at the beginning of each nine-week grading period to monitor how the program is functioning. Things to consider during the quarterly meetings are number of students attending, how to increase and manage enrollment, guest readers, rotating the reading material and raffle items, tracking the number of minutes that students are reading, and reading posters. Things to be in place to kick off EBR for the next school year are an EBR promotional campaign, times of operation and program guidelines, reading materials, personnel to run EBR, raffle items, sign-in logs and signs, EBR sign, ALA READ poster software, and floor pillows/beanbag chairs. Everyone on the EBR team plays an important role in making this program a success!

Sign-in Logs, Signs, Raffle Tickets, Raffle Container, and Raffle Items

Signing in at Early Bird Readers.

To maximize reading time, create a sign-in area for each grade level. Have sign-in forms on a clipboard for students to easily shift to a new form as the top one fills up. Simple grade-level signs can be created with a laminated 5 × 7 index card folded in half with the grade level on it. A small divided tray is handy for storing raffle tickets, pencils, and the raffle container. Raffle containers are screw-top plastic containers with a hold cut in the lid. Raffle items are trendy and seasonal school supplies such as notepads, erasers, bookmarks, pencils tops, pencils, and pens. Items must not interfere with the classroom atmosphere.

Reading Material

Select reading material: a great selection of nonfiction, graphic novels, and magazines with tubs for storage.

This is the most important part of the program! High-interest fiction and nonfiction reading materials in a variety of reading levels and formats are the key to attracting students. Graphic novels, comic books, popular fiction, nonfiction, and series titles are the heart of the program. Look at the EBR suggested reading list for ideas. Contact the local newspaper to subscribe to the "Newspapers in Education" program. This program provides multiple copies of the local newspaper free of charge. Invite the newspaper's marketing person to EBR to discuss the various sections of the newspaper so that students understand what the newspaper offers in print and online formats. If the newspaper is available online, students can read in this format too. Include audiobooks and *eBooks* as part of the EBR collection. Audiobooks in *Playaway* format are easy for students to use and reading speed can be adjusted. It is *very* important to rotate and add to the EBR collection to continue to keep attendance and interest high. Funding to support EBR reading materials is necessary for success. Grants, monies from the school budget, PTA support, local businesses, and profits from book fairs keep EBRs happy and reading throughout the year.

EBR Guidelines

Breakfast and a book.

As noted in the research chapter, successful SSR programs have structure. Here are some suggestions for a structured SSR program. You can adjust the times to fit your schedule.

Guidelines for EBR are

✦ EBR is open for silent reading **only** from 7:20 to 7:50 A.M., Monday through Friday.

✦ Doors close at 7:30 A.M., to ensure at least 20 minutes of daily SSR.

✦ Students sign in, complete raffle slip, stow jackets, and gather reading materials.

✦ NO ONE is allowed to stand up unless there is a bathroom need.

✦ Students may eat breakfast but neatness and manners must be present.

✦ Students may bring their own reading material.

✦ No homework or studying allowed, only reading.

✦ Looking up an unfamiliar word in a dictionary or thesaurus is allowed.

✦ Students are responsible for cleaning up their area when EBR is over.

EBR Daily Routine for Supervising Adults

1. Set out the EBR reading and sign-in materials and floor pillows.

2. Put the EBR sign in hallway to indicate EBR is open.

3. Set timer to allow students to know when EBR is finished.

4. Shut library door to indicate EBR is closed.

5. Supervise and read.

6. Continue reading until timer goes off.

7. Supervise students as they clean up their area and line up to be dismissed.

8. Return EBR materials to storage area and return cafeteria trays.

9. Wipe off tables.

10. Enter minutes from sign-in logs throughout the week.

Raffle Day

Raffle winners: Fancy pencils, erasers, and pens.

Raffle day is a random day during the week. It occurs at the end of an EBR session. Stop reading five minutes early on Raffle day. Students must be present to win. Gather all the raffle slips from each grade-level container and place in a large tub. Shuffle the slips well and pull 10 slips. You can determine the number of winners. Students called come and select their item. If a name is selected twice, it is discarded so that there are 10 different winners. Students quickly understand the more they attend EBR, the greater their chances of winning. Discard all old raffle slips. A new raffle begins the next day. Like the reading materials, raffle items should be rotated and desirable.

Student Reading Milestones

Recognize students throughout the year for participating in EBR program. EBR is a voluntary program, so promoting student participation is important for the program's success. EBR bulletin boards and displays near the library and school foyer demonstrate the school community's commitment to reading and academics. Record student minutes using a spreadsheet (Excel or Google Documents) that calculates the number of minutes read per session and provides totals of minutes read. A volunteer or a paraprofessional can assist with this task. It is important to enter student minutes weekly to inform students of their progress and to keep up with student recognitions. This increases motivation for attending EBR.

✦ 100 minutes read = photo of student is taken and placed on the EBR bulletin board.

✦ 500 minutes read = students select and make a decorative frame for their picture to take home.

✦ 500 minutes read = for every 500 minutes read, students receive a collectible EBR dog tag (optional).

✦ 1,000 minutes read = students have a READ poster made of them with their favorite book to be displayed in the hallway outside the library and also one to take home.

Students can re-qualify for this recognition and earn more than one READ poster. At the awards assembly at the end of the school year, students receive certificates for EBR participation. Each student's name and number of minutes read during the school year is announced. This is very impressive to all attending the awards assembly, especially parents.

Results of EBR

EBR received the first AASL Innovative Reading Award in 2007. EBR provides a daily 20–40-minute SSR voluntary session for third through sixth grades. Students in Grades 3–6 read 250,898 minutes during the 2009–2010 school year (September–May 15). Attitudes about reading changed and students felt their fluency and comprehension improved. Parents and caregivers reported improvement in their child's reading ability and interest in reading.

Student Comments about EBR

Comfortable reading with a floor pillow and Harry Potter. Floor pillows, bean bag chairs, and small futons make for comfortable reading.

Student surveys revealed that a quiet reading area and being able to self-select materials from a variety of print are motivating. Alexus reported, "I like to read here and it is not loud." Students discovered the consistent reading time allowed them to complete books previously thought to be too long or too difficult. "I am in my second Harry Potter book, I didn't think I could ever read HP because it was too long but now I have the time in Early Birds," said fourth-grader Emily. Students discovered they enjoyed reading once they were given a chance to select what they wanted to read and silently without an accompanying task. Many students reported, "feeling good about reading" and "it (EBR) has helped me know that reading is fun." When asked about their selections, students said they enjoyed animal stories, magazines such as Ranger Rick, comic books, newspapers, and graphic novels. Several students mentioned being able to read more state award books. Fourth-grade Sierra mentioned enjoying the newspaper so much that "I started a newspaper for my class, and I learned how to write horoscopes and comics from reading *The Boomerang*." Asked what they would be doing if they didn't attend EBR, students replied, "I would be late coming to school," "sitting in class being bored and listening to all kinds of loud talk," "playing on the playground," or "I would be snoring in my bed!"

Parent and Caregiver Comments about EBR

✦ "I think it helps her have intentional reading time, reinforced by her peers."

✦ "Hanna pushes me to get her there early so she can read!"

✦ "She reads faster and her reading level has increased."

✦ "We don't need to bring our child to Early Bird Readers; we feel is it a great opportunity to advance reading skills."

✦ "She has learned more words, and she tells her brothers new words" (about a student who is learning English).

✦ "I would say the time he gets to spend as an Early Bird Reader has encouraged him to read more books of his own selection."

✦ "He gets upset if he thinks he is going to be late to school and miss Early Bird Readers!"

✦ "I think having a morning group that is special is really a motivator."

✦ Asked whether their fourth-grade child's reading ability has increased through participation in EBR, the parents wrote, "We think so. For the past few years he has just barely been keeping up. Right now he just tested at grade level. We are certain that EBR has helped."

✦ Another parent described her third-grade son's attitude about EBR: "Jack would not come to school unless there was Early Bird Readers. He makes me get him up early so he can be the first one in the library. Jack doesn't like Fridays because there is not Early Bird Readers so I really have to work hard to get him to come to school." Jack read over 2,600 minutes this year during EBR!

✦ Last of all, a parent wrote, "Listing the days when there is no Early Bird Reading in advance on the school calendar would be helpful. We 'LOVE' Early Bird Reading."

End of the School Year

✦ Meet with the library committee, principal, literacy coach, and other stake-holders to plan for EBR program for the upcoming school year.

✦ Apply for grants to supplement EBR reading material and other supplies. Promote EBR with PTA, civic groups, and businesses to secure funding for reading materials. Seeking funding is an on-going activity.

✦ Contact the local newspaper for free Newspapers in Education (NIE). Order 10 copies of the local newspaper.

During the Summer

✦ Secure dish tubs or baskets to store EBR materials.

✦ Prepare a slide program to advertise EBR during the first week of school, and for PTA and donors.

✦ Prepare an EBR invitation to go home with students during the first week of school.

✦ Learn to use ALA READ poster software through the online tutorial.

✦ Visit local printer to inquire about printing the READ posters.

During Teacher Preplanning and First Week of School

✦ EBR team presents program to the faculty. Encourage teachers to promote EBR with parents and caregivers during open house.

✦ Copy and collate EBR invitations for grades three through six.

✦ Practice slideshow to be shown to students during the second library visit.

✦ Secure raffle items, raffle containers, and clipboards for sign-in.

✦ Copy EBR sign-in logs and raffle forms.

✦ Make signs for grade-level sign-in and an EBR bookworm sign.

✦ Have a digital clock visible for students in addition to traditional clock.

✦ Obtain appropriate level comic books. Students may volunteer to donate them and children's magazines.

✦ Obtain beanbag chairs and floor pillows. These items can be donated, but must be in good condition.

Second Week of School

✦ Enthusiastically present EBR slideshow to third through sixth grade classes.

✦ Send EBR invitations home with students.

✦ Ask teachers to promote EBR with students in the classroom.

✦ Place EBR announcement on school website, PTA newsletter, and hallway posters.

✦ Create an EBR bulletin board in the school foyer or outside the library.

Third Week of School

✦ Place EBR sign outside the library each morning.

✦ Set up the library for EBR.

✦ Go to the cafeteria and invite students to come to EBR with breakfast.

✦ Have student volunteers or on-duty faculty invite students to EBR as they come into school.

"Welcome to Early Bird Readers!" This sign signals EBR is open for business.

✦ Direct students to grade-level sign-in areas, stow backpacks, and find reading materials.

✦ Set timer for cleanup/ dismissal time.

✦ READ!!

✦ When the timer rings, EBR is over for the day. Students clean up their area, bus their trays to the cafeteria cart, and line up to be dismissed.

Students earned READ posters for reading 1,000 minutes.

- When the warning bell sounds, students leave for class.

- Librarian or clerk return trays to the cafeteria and wipe off tables.

- Return EBR materials to storage room. Students can assist with this task.

Additional EBR Procedures or Things I Learned along the Way

- *Raffle:* The raffle items were fancy school supplies such as bookmarks, pens, pencils, and erasers. Rotate the raffle items regularly. Be respectful of teachers and select raffle items that are not distracting in the classroom.

- *Pictures, Picture Frames, and Dog Tags:* It is very rewarding to students to be recognized on the EBR bulletin board. An adult volunteer worked with students at recess time to assemble the frames. A variety of dog tags were ordered so that students were able to create a "collection" of the tags over the school year. The glow-in-the-dark dog tags were popular.

- *READ posters:* Investing in the READ software is expensive, but very worthwhile. Learn to use the software long before a student reaches 1,000 minutes. Practice making READ posters with faculty. See if any faculty or parent is a photography buff, knows Photoshop, and would be willing to help and teach you. Find a local printer who will print the posters (11 × 17) for a nominal fee or as a donation. A sign near the READ poster stating, "Poster printing donated by Kinkos-FedEX" recognizes the business for their donation. At the end of the year, write a thank you note to the printer and other donors. Include them in an end-of-the-year article in the PTA newsletter and on school website.

- *Reading Logs and Statistics:* Stay current on reading log tallies of students' minutes read. It is important to recognize students as soon as they reach a goal. Your technology coordinator can assist in setting up a spread sheet (Excel or Google Documents) that allows you to enter students by grade and will automatically calculate their daily minutes read. Adult volunteers or high-school students needing service hours are very helpful at entering minutes read and tallying them. Keeping statistics on number of participating students, grade-level information, minutes read is a valuable tool for library reports, grants, and for obtaining donations. Student surveys, parent surveys, and photographs are also important in explaining the program to parents, administrators, and school faculty. Recognize students at the end-of-the year awards assembly with a certificate and number of minutes read during the school year. The audience of parents and caregivers are always impressed at the number of minutes students read before school.

- EBR can be run at middle school following the same structure. Adjust reading material and raffle items for older students.

Early Bird Readers
Your Child Is Invited!!

Who:

Where:

When:

Why: To promote recreational reading, allow students extra time for daily reading practice, and provide a quiet place to read.

Have your child join us for Early Bird Reading. Students may bring their breakfast to the library, eat, and begin to read silently from a selection of magazines, newspapers, graphic novels (colorful books with word bubbles), books, and audiobooks. Students that eat breakfast at home may bypass the cafeteria and come directly to the library to begin reading at ___ A.M. Students that are driven to school may report to Early Bird Readers as early as ___!! Students must be in the library by ___ A.M.

We will begin on _____.

If you have any questions, please call _____.

Sincerely,

_____, librarian

Early Bird Readers Reading Materials

Book Series and Publishers

Nonfiction

Bearport—http://www.bearportpublishing.com/

Capstone—http://www.capstonepub.com/

National Geographic—http://shop.nationalgeographic.com/ngs/category/books/kids-books-and-atlases?categoryLevelId=A001

Dorling Kindersley Books—http://us.dk.com/static/cs/us/11/childrens/intro.html

Scholastic—http://www.scholastic.com/teachers/

Lerner—www.lernerbooks.com

Peachtree Publishers—http://peachtree-online.com/index.php/books/search

Graphic Novels

Cooperative Children's Book Center Recommended Titles for Children and Teens—http://www.education.wisc.edu/ccbc/books/detailListBooks.asp?idBookLists=192

The Eisner Awards—http://www.comic-con.org/cci/cci_eisnersfaq.shtml

School Library Journal (reviewed and recommended graphic novels)—http://www.slj.com/search-results/?q=graphic%20novels

Early Bird Readers Sign In

Date	Name	Time	Teacher

Early Bird Readers Survey

Parents: Early Bird Readers is a voluntary reading program that runs daily from 7:30–8:10 A.M. Students read silently from books, graphic novels, newspapers, and magazines. Please comment below on the Early Bird Readers program. Thank you.

Has your child discussed Early Bird Readers at home? Explain.

Has Early Bird Readers increased your child's reading ability? Discuss.

Has the Early Bird Readers program increased your child's interest in or motivation to read? Explain.

Additional comments.

 From *For the Love of Reading: Guide to K–8 Reading Promotions* by Nancy L. Baumann. Santa Barbara, CA: Libraries Unlimited. Copyright © 2013.

Name_____

Teacher_____

Name_____

Teacher_____

Name_____

Teacher_____

Name_____

Teacher_____

Name_____

Teacher_____

Name_____

Teacher_____

Name_____

Teacher_____

Name_____

Teacher_____

Name_____

Teacher_____

Name_____

Teacher_____

 **Notes**

CHAPTER 3

Reading Lunch is really good. You get to listen to a really good book and eat your lunch at the same time.

—Maria, fifth grade

And you get to sit with your friends.

—Ana, fifth grade

PURPOSE

To provide a daily read-aloud time for students during their lunch break.

GOALS

To provide consistent read-aloud sessions for students outside the classroom schedule.

To promote recreational reading.

To improve listening and comprehension skills.

To introduce students to a variety of genres, classics, award-winning literature, and series.

To provide informal discussion of literary techniques as prescribed in Common Core State Standards (CCSS) and American Association of School Librarians (AASL) standards.

To promote the congeniality of a book group.

To alleviate lunchroom boredom and noise.

MATERIALS

A variety of vetted read-aloud fiction and nonfiction

Book talks and book trailers

Slideshow to promote reading lunch

Reading Lunch attendance log

Reading Lunch request slips

Toweling and disinfectant cleaner

Small carpet sweeper

Implementation of Reading Lunch

Preparing for Reading Lunch is a continuous project. The first step is to consult with your principal and school-governing body to propose Reading Lunch. Discuss the purpose and benefits of hosting Reading Lunch. Explain Reading Lunch rules and a procedure for getting students from their classroom to the lunchroom for lunch pickup and to the library without a commotion.

Book Selection

Book selection is an ongoing project. Discovering titles that qualify for Reading Lunch is an important and pleasurable task. Reading reviews, recommending booklists, participating in professional webinars and blogs, and browsing appropriate websites are helpful in discovering a variety of genres, lengths, and listening levels. A variety of genres is a must and helps meet CCSS and AASL standards. Finding literature with rich language, exciting and memorable characters, and layered plots are on the Reading Lunch wish list. Action-filled adventures, mysteries that slowly unravel, and a variety of characters from diverse cultures are also "musts." Books we want students to read but they won't pick up also find their way onto the Reading Lunch list. Use reviews in School Library Journal, Horn Book, and Jim Trelease's Read Aloud Handbook for suggestions. Other ideas for read-alouds can come from International Reading Association's Children's Choices and Young Adult Choices Booklists, and recommended lists from Young Adults Library Service Association (YALSA, a division of American Library Association (ALA)), Association of Library Services for Children (ALSC, a division of ALA), and LM_Net.

For a year-round Reading Lunch program, use eight novels per grade level and four books a semester. In small schools, if two grades are combined for lunch, Reading Lunch works for fifth and sixth grades or third and fourth grades. In larger schools, read to one grade level at a time. Sometimes, a double session is necessary with popular titles. The same book is read twice in order to satisfy the number of requests.

An example of Reading Lunch titles for a semester for fifth and sixth grades:

Book 1 = *Maximum Ride: The Angel Experiment*—Patterson

Book 2 = *Invisible Lines*—Amato

Book 3 = *The Mostly True Story of Homer P. Figg*—Philbrick

Book 4 = *Cracker: The Best Dog in Viet Nam*—Kadohata

Read and reread the books you feel will work for you. Humor, drama, adventure, interesting plots, and memorable characters are all important to be eligible for a Reading Lunch selection. Once you have made selections, search for book trailers or create your own. Write an introduction to Reading Lunch to explain the program using a slideshow. Introduce the choices. Create interest! The book talks must be so intriguing that students will be begging to come to Reading Lunch. Aim your book talks at the most reluctant or resistant reader. This is the clientele you want to attract. Short annotations of the Reading Lunch books can be included in the PTA newsletter and the school website. Next, schedule visits with classroom teachers to present Reading Lunch, book talks/book trailers, and sign up. This can also be accomplished during a class visit to the library. About 20–30 minutes is needed. Tally results from student request slips and send teachers a list of Reading Lunch attendees and a date to begin.

Reading Lunch Schedule

Initially getting students from the classroom to the lunchroom to get lunch and then on to the library for Reading Lunch seems like a monumental task. Once a procedure is in place, getting students to the library quickly for Reading Lunch is not a problem. On the day Reading Lunch is to begin, place a sign with an enlarged copy of the book jacket and a message "Reading Lunch begins today at 12:20" outside the library. Post the attendees list alongside the poster as a reminder. Schedule an announcement for morning announcements and e-mail teachers to remind students. Students easily come regularly once the book has begun. Students who bring lunch from home come directly from their classroom. Others will go through the lunch line and hurry to the library. Accommodations such as having Reading Lunch students proceed first through the lunch line for their grade is helpful. Place napkins and wet wipes on the tables to help with neatness. Expect to wait about five to six minutes for students to arrive before reading. Students may move chairs to add more places to a table, but are responsible to return them. Visiting quietly and eating until you begin reading is acceptable. Have a student volunteer check off names as students arrive. Keeping attendance is helpful for statistics for end-of-the-year library reporting and to keep track of students. It is helpful knowing if someone is absent, working on homework, or not coming. A rule of Reading Lunch is students must attend daily unless they have an excused absence or homework to complete. Reading Lunch is not a drop-in activity. Another library rule is acceptance, and students know to welcome someone who wants to sit with them. Reading Lunch rules are reviewed at the beginning of each book. Reading Lunch rules are eating politely, listening while the book is being read, eating neatly, and cleaning your space.

While they are waiting, encourage students to make predictions on what will happen in today's reading. Use a whiteboard or chart paper to write predictions and comments about the characters. This creates a unique story map that students revisit daily. Teachers often stop by to check the story map as they hear the books being discussed in the classroom. Begin with a brief recap of the story or a prediction. This keeps the students alert for developments in the story. Read with dramatic expression so that listeners can "see" the story unfolding "like a movie" in their heads. Verbal sound effects can easily be added with you making "squeaky doors" noises, booms, screaming voices, and weeping. This creates atmosphere and makes it easy for listeners to insert themselves into the story. Listeners must be quiet while the story is being read. No one is allowed to get up, throw away trash, or gesture. The number one focus is on listening. Read for 20 minutes on Monday through Thursday. Fridays are reserved for students to get together with friends who aren't attending Reading Lunch. Students are expected to attend Reading Lunch if they have reserved a spot. Excused absences are illness, appointments, meetings, and homework. Occasionally, a student finds the book not interesting and requests to be dismissed. However, they can't return to Reading Lunch until the next book starts. Students are dismissed for excessive talking and distracting behavior while the book is being read. Allow for three minutes at the end of Reading Lunch for comments and cleanup. Have a trash container available and have students check around them and on the floor for wrappers. All chairs must be returned to original places. Clean off tables and chairs with a disinfectant spray as students are leaving. Student volunteers can help with this task.

Reading Lunch buddies.

When you reach the final chapter of the current Reading Lunch book, remind students the next book will start soon. Check to see if there are any openings for seats in the new book and invite anyone who is interested to sign up for a spot. Many students are hooked on Reading Lunch as an alternative to the lunchroom and listening to a new read-aloud. Alert teachers on the beginning of a new book with an e-mail reminder and a listener list. Post the new book's enlarged book jacket on display outside the library with the listener list.

Results of Reading Lunch

Reading Lunch is an integral part of a library program. Students anxiously await the beginning of a new session and book. It is one of the few programs that is free, highly beneficial, and not tied to testing. It provides an opportunity for students to be read to regularly. Reading Lunch creates a literary community for its listeners and promotes a reading habit. It stimulates imagination and conversation. Another benefit is listening to a variety of genres. During the school year, participants will be able to hear a mystery, an adventure, an informational title, a realistic and historical fiction, a science fiction, and a fantasy. Award winning books such as Newbery Award titles are selected for their high quality and rich language. Students find themselves discussing Reading Lunch books with friends and family. In addition, students use reading skills such as story mapping, character traits, and prediction during Reading Lunch. The whiteboard or chart paper in the library is used to record their opinions and is updated daily.

Ready for Reading Lunch to begin.

Students relish feeling part of a reading community and enjoy hearing and informally discussing books with peers. Reading Lunch provides a venue for popular books that some students really want to read but find too difficult. All students can enjoy the book as they all can listen. Special needs students, especially students with autism, appreciate the quiet friendly atmosphere of Reading Lunch. Last of all, there are fewer students to supervise in the lunchroom, students eat more or most of their lunches, and sometimes parents will join their child in Reading Lunch.

Additional Results

✦ Students listen to books with more difficult text and vocabulary than they can read themselves.

✦ Students use creative skills to create illustrations of what they are hearing.

- Students eat more of their lunch as they are eating and listening.
- Students become interested in trying to read books they previously felt were too difficult or boring.
- Students purchase the Reading Lunch title and follow along or read ahead but do not spoil the book for others.
- Students have an opportunity to hear State Award book nominees resulting in more voting.
- Teachers are happy that students are being read to as they don't have time in their schedule or don't know what to read.
- Listening to a book is a desirable activity and good practice.
- Parents comment they are happy about their child participating in Reading Lunch as their child discusses the book daily at dinner.
- Parents read the Reading Lunch book selections after hearing comments from their child.
- Parents attend Reading Lunch with their child if they are eating lunch with the child at school, learning the importance of reading aloud.
- Students create story maps and illustrations of the book on their own as the book is being read.
- "Safe" nonthreatening environment for all students.
- Students eat their entire lunches and learn about good lunches from other listeners.

Step-by-Step Preparation for Reading Lunch

All Year Long

- Search out books to read for Reading Lunch.

Three Months Out (May)

- Prepare book talks for selected books for the upcoming school year. Find or create book trailers to accompany book talks.

One Month Out (July)

- Decide which four books will be used during the first semester. Be prepared to begin Reading Lunch during the second week of school.
- Prepare book request forms.

Teacher Preplanning

✦ Schedule classroom visits to introduce the program and books.

✦ Make a large color copy (11 × 17) of each title and laminate them.

One Week Out (First Week of School)

✦ Visit classrooms, introduce Reading Lunch, and perform book talks and show trailers. Hold up the book cover posters when talking about the books. Attach book talk to the backs of the posters before laminating.

✦ Have students complete request slips.

✦ Tally the request slips and make attendance list for the books. Include the start date. E-mail the list to the teachers and the principal. Request teachers post the list in the classroom.

✦ Post the list outside the library next to the book cover poster.

Reading Lunch Begins

✦ Send an e-mail to teachers to remind students about Reading Lunch.

✦ Submit an announcement about Reading Lunch for morning announcements.

✦ Complete the attendance sheet with student's names and date.

✦ Place napkins and wet wipes on library tables. Set out trash container.

✦ Welcome students and have a volunteer check off names.

✦ Let the reading begin!!

Reading Lunch Attendance Sheet

Name/Date																						

 From *For the Love of Reading: Guide to K–8 Reading Promotions* by Nancy L. Baumann. Santa Barbara, CA: Libraries Unlimited. Copyright © 2013.

Reading Lunch Book Suggestions

Maximum Ride: The Angel Experiment—Patterson

A Single Shard—Park

Peace, Locomotion—Woodson

Esperanza Rising—Ryan

Sammy Keyes and the Wild Things—Van Draanen

Scat—Hiaasen

Mrs. Frisby and the Rats of NIMH—O'Brien

The Ghost of Fossil Glen—DeFelice

Poppy—Avi

Al Capone Does My Shirts—Choldenko

Kensuke's Kingdom—Morpurgo

Aliens Ate My Homework—Coville

The Righteous Revenge of Artemis Bonner—Myers

Peter and the Starcatchers—Barrie

Wild Girl—Giff

A View from the Cherry Tree—Roberts

Schooled—Korman

Crispin—Avi

The Tale of Desperaux—DiCamillo

Shiloh—Naylor (trilogy)

Peak—Smith

Savvy—Law

Kavik, the Wolf Dog—Morey

The Absolutely True Story or How I Visited Yellowstone Park... Roberts

All the Lovely Bad Ones—Hahn

Three on Three—Walters

A Dog Named Kitty—Wallace

Getting Air—Gutman

Fablehaven—Mull

Dealing with Dragons—Wrede

Found—Haddix

Ruby Holler—Creech

The Hunger Games—Collins

Trapped in Death Cave—Wallace

Crash—Spinelli

Deep and Dark and Dangerous—Hahn

Bud not Buddy—Curtis

The False Prince—Nielsen

Gregor the Overlander—Collins

The Pinballs—Byers

The Haymeadow—Paulsen

A Long Way from Chicago—Peck

Football Hero—Green

Earthquake Terror—Kehret

The Homework Machine—Gutman

Fever, 1793—Anderson

Travel Team—Lupica

Loch—Zindel

Cryptid Hunters—Smith

The Grand Escape—Naylor

Rules—Lord

How to Steal a Dog—O'Connor

Ark Angel—Horowitz

Heart of a Shepherd—Parry

Everything for a Dog—Martin

When the Mountain Meets the Moon—Lin

The Mostly True Adventures of Homer P. Figg—Philbrick

Listen!—Tolan

Taking Sides—Soto

White Water—Petersen

The Small Adventure of Popeye and Elvis—O'Connor

The One and Only Ivan—Applegate

Summer of the Gypsy Moths—Pennypacker

Liar and Spy—Stead

Shipwreck at the Bottom of the World—Armstrong

Jinx—Blackwood

P.S. Be Eleven—Williams-Garcia

Escape From Mr. Lemoncello's Library—Grabenstein

One Crazy Summer—Williams-Garcia

Hattie Ever After—Larson

Invisible Lines—Amato

Cracker!—Kadohata

A Dog's Life—Martin

When You Reach Me—Stead

Candy Shop Wars—Mull

The Million Dollar Shot—Gutman

11 Birthdays—Maas

Paint the Wind—Ryan

Mysterious Benedict Society—Stewart

Three Times Lucky—Turnage

Wonder—Palacio

Starry River of the Sky—Lin

Amelia Lost—Fleming

Doll Bones—Black

The Thing About Luck—Kadohata

Hold Fast—Blue Balliett

Hattie Big Sky—Larson

 From *For the Love of Reading: Guide to K–8 Reading Promotions* by Nancy L. Baumann. Santa Barbara, CA: Libraries Unlimited. Copyright © 2013.

Reading Lunch

Name_____

Teacher_____

1st Choice_____

2nd Choice_____

3rd Choice_____

Reading Lunch

Name_____

Teacher_____

1st Choice_____

2nd Choice_____

3rd Choice_____

From *For the Love of Reading: Guide to K–8 Reading Promotions* by Nancy L. Baumann. Santa Barbara, CA: Libraries Unlimited. Copyright © 2013.

 **Notes**

CHAPTER 4

My daughter absolutely loved Mock Newbery. She became excited about the Award and being able to vote for those books even though it was on their own level, even though it didn't count. It was a great thing for them to be involved in.

—Nicole, parent

PURPOSE

To promote reading and discussion of high-quality literature while following the John Newbery Medal Award guidelines for evaluation.

GOALS

To read and discuss a minimum of six titles selected as "Newbery worthy" through professional reviewing sources such as Horn Book, School Library Journal, and BookList.

To involve students in high-level discussion through comparing and contrasting characters, settings, plots, theme, and author's purpose as prescribed in American Association of School Librarians (AASL) Standards for 21st-Century Learners and Common Core State Standards.

To develop comprehension and reasoning skills leading to forming an opinion, understanding different points of view, and applying acquired information to everyday life situations as prescribed in AASL Standards for 21st-Century Learners and Common Core State Standards.

To expand vocabulary.

To promote recreational reading.

To read, discuss, and develop an appreciation for a variety of genres.

To use social networking for additional discussion.

Implementation of MNBC

First Steps

Mock Newbery Book Club (MNBC) can be organized in several ways:

+ Readers read a group of preselected titles and discuss one book per meeting. Discussion invites evaluation and comparison between titles as more books are completed.

+ Readers choose and read independently from a collection of "Newbery Possibility" titles. Books are presented and "book talked" at meetings by individual readers. Questions and comments from other members are posed as each reader presents the book he or she has read. Readers present several books during the meeting if time allows.

+ Readers read from a set number of the same titles for discussion and present additional titles self-selected from a list of "Newbery Possibilities" given to readers throughout the MNBC.

Each version is fun for readers and results in book promotion and lively discussion.

Selecting the Books

Deciding which books to read is the first step. The *Heavy Medal Blog* on the *School Library Journal* site provides a beginning list shortly after the Newbery Award is named. The *Eva Perry Mock Newbery Book Club Blog* (Apex, NC) and *Allen County Public Library Mock Newbery Blog* (Fort Wayne, IN) are also reliable sites for suggestions. On these sites, teens, young adults, and librarians are reading, discussing, and blogging about possible Newbery choices. Join the blog on Goodreads.com, *Let the Hunt Begin*. All of these sites provide possible titles to use for MNBC. Take an online class from Association of Library Services to Children (ALSC) on the history of the Newbery Award. Purchase the *Mock Newbery Handbook* from ALSC. The class and manual will provide important historical information about the Newbery Medal and sharpen your book discussion skills. The manual provides historical Newbery information, procedures, and forms.

Acquiring the Books

Finding funding for the books can be a challenging task. However, many businesses are interested in supporting a literacy project. Presentation of the project is key to raising funds. Invite a local bookstore or business to sponsor titles during the Mock Newbery session. Services that involve children such as dentists, orthodontists, and pediatricians are very supportive of projects. Businesses such as banks and credit unions often have a line in their budget for community service and support literacy projects. Prepare a packet explaining the club, purposes, benefits, who is involved, cost of a hardcover book, amount needed, book reviews, and a parent information form. Use slides or photographs from previous club meetings. Include your business card in the information packet. Sometimes, the merchant you approach is not able to help but knows of another organization that can. Other sources for funding include grants, PTA, principal's fund, book fair profits, civic organizations, and parent donations through vendors. Collect advance reader copies when attending professional conferences. Write publishers and request advance reader copies. The MNBC facilitator at the *Eva Perry Public Library* writes to publishers on library letterhead to request titles for the group. The public library and interlibrary loan are also good resources for book acquisition.

Collaborators

Involving additional facilitators is important. Teachers, librarians, university students, and retirees contribute greatly to discussions and ensure meetings run smoothly. They can take over tasks such as member sign-in, book return, and checkout. Training of volunteers is crucial. Again, an informational packet and orientation is important for success.

Procedure

Begin promoting MNBC when the school year starts. Let everyone know about the MNBC book group. Appeal to audiences to become part of "competing" to discover this year's John Newbery Award book. In the school setting, promotion includes classroom visits, promotional posters, blurbs on the school website, and in the PTA newsletter. For groups meeting at public libraries, promotion can be done through the library's website and newsletter. Families can come in to the library or call to register. Classroom visits to schools to promote the book group are motivating to potential members. School groups can meet during lunch, before or after school. After school or late afternoon works well for groups meeting at public libraries. Meeting rooms sometimes dictate the time and day. Provide handouts for parents and caregivers explaining the purpose of the book discussion, the Newbery Award, and a reading contract. Include the date for the registration form to be returned to the library. This provides an idea for the number of members. Plan to hold the initial meeting shortly after Labor Day. Scheduling eight sessions every other week works well with voting in late December. In a school setting, students enjoy discussing the books until right before the award is announced. Settle on a plan to remind participants of meetings with a phone call, e-mail, or both. Prepare for the group to correspond or update one another through a blog. Many school districts provide student accounts for assignments and discussions. Public libraries host members-only blogs for discussion purposes. Plan to watch the awards ceremony held at American Library Association's (ALA's) Mid-Winter Conference in January. Students at schools can watch the ceremony in the library. Winners are announced via live streaming over the ALA website. It is exciting and suspenseful.

Step-by-Step Planning for MNBC

Six Months Out

✦ Meet with adults who will be collaborating in the MNBC. Topics to be discussed are promotional materials and procedures, number of participants, meeting dates, and book selection and checkout.

✦ Prepare promotional information for Fall Public Library Newsletter and website.

✦ E-mail adult collaborators to discuss titles to be used for MNBC.

Two Months Out

✦ Meet with adult collaborators to decide on meeting room. Final discussion on book selection. Order books and review MNBC promotional materials.

✦ Prepare book talks and locate book trailers or create original trailers.

✦ Check with the technology department creating a members-only blog.

One Month Out

✦ Finalize book talks. Prepare guided question bookmarks and discussion questions for selected titles. (Hint: Check author and publisher websites for downloadable discussion guides and book trailers.)

✦ Prepare presentation for classroom visits.

✦ Prepare informational packets about the John Newbery Medal and book group guidelines for adult collaborators and members. Use the *ALSC Mock Newbery Manual* and *The John Newbery Medal* homepage on the *ALA* website. Review this information with adult facilitators.

Three Weeks Out

✦ Schedule class visits or school visits with teachers and librarians via e-mail or phone calls. Alert them to the information on the library website or in library newsletter.

✦ Practice MNBC presentation for classroom visits.

Two Weeks Out

✦ Promotional visits to classrooms and member sign-up.

✦ Check out meeting space for room setup.

✦ Order or purchase snacks. Supplies include napkins, wet wipes, and tissues. (Hint: Sam's Club has large boxes of individually wrapped snacks, juice boxes, and small bottled water.)

✦ Check on status of book order. Decide the order books will be read.

✦ Meet with technology department for blog demonstration.

One Week Out

✦ Finalize meeting room arrangement.

✦ Prepare MNBC notebook for attendance and book circulation. Store extra bookmarks in notebook.

✦ Acquire a stopwatch for discussion timing.

✦ Prepare handouts for parents and caregivers with book reviews, time of meetings, and dates.

✦ Finalize and copy member handouts with book group guidelines, Newbery information, and guidelines.

First Meeting

◆ Greet members at the door of the meeting room. As members arrive, introduce yourself and direct them to the snacks.

◆ Invite members to sign in and make a nametag. When you feel everyone is present, ask members to introduce themselves. It can be as simple as their name, favorite book or genre, and favorite Newbery book.

◆ Once introductions are complete, welcome them to the annual Mock Newbery Book Group, where "kids" choose the winners!! Pass out the information on book group guidelines (see example) and Newbery history. Review the guidelines for book discussion and decide which guidelines will work for this group. Ask members what they know about the John Newbery Medal and books. Present a brief history of the medal.

◆ Have the six titles to be discussed on display during the Mock Newbery session. Briefly book talk each title. Have students check out the first title to be read. Number each book in the front cover. Record the member's name and number of book in the Newbery notebook. Provide members with a bookmark of guided questions to think about while reading. Members can write comments on the bookmark with page numbers of important passages. Include blog information on the bookmark.

◆ Pass out a second bookmark with the Newbery criteria for the medal so that members can consider this as they read the books.

Club members signing it at a meeting.

◆ Next, assemble students for a group picture with the books. Ask for any questions from the group. Allow members to begin reading.

◆ Adjourn at designated time. Thank everyone for coming. Pass out MNBC informational materials to parents and caregivers. Make sure members meet their ride home. Clean up the meeting room.

Meeting 2

◆ Set up meeting room and snacks. Place the Newbery notebook on a table for members to sign in as they arrive.

◆ Be at the door to greet members as they arrive. Allow for some socializing and eating before getting started.

✦ Reintroduce one another and ask for questions. Ask for timer volunteer and provide them a stopwatch.

✦ Begin discussions by asking for reactions to the book. Use the guided questions from the bookmark to initiate discussion. Ask if anyone discovered an interesting paragraph or character. An informal vote can be taken with "this is the best book I ever read," "an ok book," or "not distinguished." Ask members to support their comments. Voting can also be recorded by using die-cut figures on a poster.

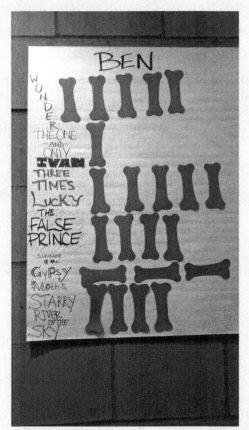

Keeping track of Mock Newbery preferences.

✦ Introduce the next book with a short but engaging book talk. Pass out guided question bookmarks and books. Copy them on another color of paper. Store the extra bookmarks in the Newbery notebook.

✦ Record second book's copy number and member's name in the Newbery notebook.

✦ Collect the first week's book and bookmarks from members. Cross off the returned books in the Newbery notebook. Keep the bookmarks in a folder for future discussions.

✦ Invite members to present any additional books they feel merits Newbery status.

✦ Allow time for questions and then begin reading.

✦ Adjourn at the designated time. Thank everyone for coming. Make sure members meet their ride home. Clean up the meeting room.

Meetings 3–6

The rest of the meetings will run with this format.

Meeting 7: Voting Preparation

✦ Greet members, invite them to sign in, and pick up snacks.

✦ Discuss the final book using the procedure from the prior meetings.

✦ Have members check in the final book and bookmarks.

✦ Invite members to present any additional books they feel merit Newbery status.

- Using the Newbery voting handout, discuss the voting procedure for the Newbery Medal and ballots. Provide about 15 minutes at the end of this meeting for this task.

- Adjourn at the designated time. Thank everyone for coming. Make sure they meet their ride home. Clean up the meeting room.

Meeting 8: Voting and Final Meeting

- Greet members, invite them to sign in, and pick up some snacks. (Hint: Serving pizza at the last meeting is popular with participants.)

- Discuss the merits of their top choices. Distribute the guided question bookmarks for members review as they discuss the books.

- Pass out ballots to members for voting. Tally votes while members socialize, snack, and complete a survey. The survey will provide information from participants in order to plan for the next year.

- Announce the results. Take photographs of the members and winning books.

- Thank everyone for participating and remind them about the live streaming of the ALSC awards at Mid-Winter Conference.

- An e-mail will be sent to members to remind them to watch for the announcements.

A ballot, pizza, and good books.

- Discuss interest in a Mock Newbery reunion in January to meet, socialize, and discuss the winning titles.

- Adjourn at the designated time. Thank everyone for coming. Make sure they meet their ride home. Clean up the meeting room.

After the MNBC Is Completed

- Review surveys with adult facilitators. Prepare a statement for the end-of-the-year library report from the survey.

- Write thank you notes to volunteers and sponsors. Enclose a photograph of the MNBC group.

- ✦ Submit an article about the MNBC to the PTA newsletter, school website, school district website, and local newspaper. Include any business or organization that donated funds for books and snacks.

- ✦ Report on the book group's activities at PTA or Youth Services Board Meeting. Request funding or partial funding for next year's MNBC.

Tips

Discussion can occasionally slow down. Here are some activities to use to perk up the group:

- ✦ Have members draw prepared questions (Appendix) from a hat and answer. Rotate drawing questions around the group.

- ✦ Play "Hangman" using words from the books read. Go around to each member asking for a letter.

- ✦ Play "20 Questions" using "people," "places," or "things" from the books read.

- ✦ Play "Who am I?" or "Who is my partner?" Characters from the books read are placed on adhesive nametags and placed on members' backs. Members walk around and ask three "yes" or "no" questions to others to guess who they are. In "Who is my partner," members must discover who they are through questioning and then locate their partner. For example, if a member discovers he is "Charlotte" then he must locate the member who is wearing the nametag "Wilbur" from *Charlotte's Web*.

Results of MNBC

Members of MNBC reported in surveys that they "enjoyed being part of a group discussing similar books" and "liked the choice of books and voting". Several members mentioned "liking the snacks and talking about books with friends." Others wrote they "liked having older members in the group and listening to what they said during the discussions." Additional responses were:

- ✦ Enjoyed the in-depth discussions that didn't happen at school.

- ✦ Read selections they normally wouldn't choose.

- ✦ Liked comparing the books using the Newbery guidelines to vote. "I couldn't just say I liked the book, I had to give reasons to support my views," said one member.

Invitation to Join the Heavy Medal Book Discussion

Mock Newbery

(Your Library)

Dear Parents and Readers,

Join the Heavy Medal Mock Newbery Book Discussion beginning in September and be part of the discussion to select the best book of the year. The discussion will be based on the Newbery Award that is given annually by the American Library Association for the most distinguished American children's book (from birth to age 14) published the previous year. This provides a wide range of reading levels and subject matter. Participants will read six selections, discuss them, and vote for the ones they think should win the award.

Facilitator

Readers: Participants must be in Grades 4–7 and be committed to reading and discussing the selections.

When:

Dates:

Book List:

What parents can do:

✦ We depend on you to be involved with the books your child will read. The books on the discussion list have earned "Recommended" and "Starred Reviews" from professional library journals.

✦ Children differ in their readiness for particular kinds of books, and you, as parents, know what is appropriate for your own child to read.

✦ Please look at the books your child brings home; better yet, read and discuss them together!

✦ Please help by accepting responsibility for the books your child is reading.

✦ We need your permission for your child to participate in the discussion group at the (your library) library twice a month from 4:30 to 5:30 P.M.

Parent Permission Form

Mock Newbery Discussion Group

I have read and understood the information in this invitation and give my child, _____

_____, the permission to participate in the Mock Newbery Book Group.

Signed:_____Date:_____

Address:_____Phone:_____

Parent e-mail:_____

Student Contract for Mock Newbery Discussion

I hereby agree to read the six selected books between (date) and (date). I will complete an evaluation form for each book read in order to facilitate group discussion and voting for my favorite choice. I also agree to attend a minimum of six book discussions in order to participate in the final voting and enjoy a pizza snack in celebration.

Signed_____ Date_____

Heavy Medal Mock Newbery Survey

✦ Tell us about your favorite part of the Mock Newbery Book Group. Explain.

✦ How did you enjoy the snacks? Any suggestions for additional types of snacks?

✦ Explain how you feel about the book choices. Was six enough books to read?

✦ The *Mock Newbery Blog* allowed our group to make comments about the books. Did you use the blog? Why or why not?

✦ Did you learn about new authors while attending the Heavy Medal Book Club? Who? Are you interested in reading additional books by that author?

✦ Would you be interested in attending Heavy Medal Mock Newbery Book Discussion next year? Explain.

 From *For the Love of Reading: Guide to K–8 Reading Promotions* by Nancy L. Baumann. Santa Barbara, CA: Libraries Unlimited. Copyright © 2013.

Mock Newbery Ballot

December 19, 2012

Title	First Place (4 points)	Second Place (3 points)	Third Place (2 points)	Total
Wonder by R.J. Palacio				
Three Times Lucky by Sheila Turnage				
The False Prince by Jennifer Nielsen				
The One and Only Ivan by K.A. Applegate				
The Summer of the Gypsy Moths by Sarah Pennypacker				
Starry River of the Sky by Grace Lin				

Mock Newbery Book Presentation

Your mission: To present to the group why you feel your choice is worthy of the John Newbery Medal.

Here's What You Will Do!

◆ Prepare to talk to the group for 2–3 minutes about why your choice is worthy of the Newbery Medal.

◆ Things to consider when thinking about all the books you read:

❑ Is the book well organized? Did you have to reread parts to figure out what was going on in the book?

❑ Does the book have a clear beginning, middle, and end? Did the story hold your interest or was the plot predictable? Did you want to keep reading it or thought about it when you weren't reading.

❑ Are the characters well developed? Are you able to imagine what they look like? Do you feel like you know them? Do the characters act their age?

❑ Are items in the story accurate? For example, a cell phone appearing in a story like the "The False Prince."

❑ Is the style consistent throughout the entire book? For example, in "Ivan," the story was told with minimal language and through Ivan's voice. Did "Ivan" carry through with the minimal language and short chapters throughout the book?

◆ You can write or word process your notes and read from them.

Thank you! If you have questions, send me a note on the *Mock Newbery Blog*.

 From *For the Love of Reading: Guide to K–8 Reading Promotions* by Nancy L. Baumann. Santa Barbara, CA: Libraries Unlimited. Copyright © 2013.

BARNETT SHOALS NEWBERY BOOK CLUB LOG

NAME _Erik_ GRADE _4_ HOMEROOM _Ravenell_

Date	Title	Test Score	Read I Or T	Test Verification
8/31	The View from Saturday	90%	I	9-1-06
9/14	Ginger Pye	90%	I	9-15-06 NB
9/18	Dear Mr. Henshaw	100%	I	9-18-06
9/27	Holes	90%	I	9-28-06
10/3	The Tale of Despereaux	100%	I	10-3-06
11/13	Bud, Not Buddy	100%	T	11-13-06
11/16	Mrs. Frisby and the rats of NIMH	100%	I	11-16-06 NB
11/30	Shiloh	100%	I	11-30-06
12/7	Criss Cross	100%	I	NB 12-7-06
12/11	Onion John	100%	I	NB 12/11/06

For a blank Newbery Book Club Log template, see page 134.

BARNETT SHOALS NEWBERY BOOK CLUB LOG

NAME _Amani_ GRADE _5_ HOMEROOM _Wood_

Date	Title	Test Score	Read I Or T	Test Verification
9/5/06	Criss Cross	90	I	9-5-06
8/12/06	The Witch of blackbird pond	100	I	NB 9-21-06
9/21	Caddie Woodlawn	100	I	NB 9-21-06
9/27	Thimble Summer	90	I	30-2-01
10/2	I, Juan de Pareja	80	I	202-01
10/23	Bridge to terabithia	100	I	NB 1023 06
11/6/06	Mrs. frisby and the rats of NIMH	100	I	NB 11-6-06
11/13/06	Miss. Hickory	80	I	11-13-06
11/26/06	It's Like This, cat	80	I	11-27-06
2/2/07	A Single Shard	100	I	40-t-t

For a blank Newbery Book Club Log template, see page 134.

 From *For the Love of Reading: Guide to K–8 Reading Promotions* by Nancy L. Baumann. Santa Barbara, CA: Libraries Unlimited. Copyright © 2013.

BARNETT SHOALS NEWBERY BOOK CLUB LOG

NAME _Guillermo_ GRADE _4_ HOMEROOM _R-4_

Date	Title	Test Score	Read I Or T	Test Verification
9/11	The Whipping boy	100%	I	9.11.06
9/11	Mrs.Frisby and the	90%	I	9.11.06
9/21	Dear Mr. Henshaw	80%	I	9.21.06
9/21	Onion John	100%	I	9.21.06
9/22	The Tale of Des.	100%	I	9-22-06 NB
9/26	Shiloh	100%	I	9-26-06
9/27	The white Stag	80%	I	NB 9-27-06
10/26	Carry on, Mr.Bowditch	90%	I	10-26-06 NB
11/13	Bud not Buddy	100%	I	11-13-06
11/28	Witch of BlackBirdpond,The	100%	I	NB

For a blank Newbery Book Club Log template, see page 134.

BARNETT SHOALS NEWBERY BOOK CLUB LOG

NAME _Yuge Xiao_   GRADE _4_ HOMEROOM _Cunningham_

Date	Title	Test Score	Read I Or T	Test Verification
2/26/07	The trumpeter of krakow	100%	I	NB 2-26-07
2/28/07	Onion John	90%	I	NB 2-28-07
3/5/07	Shells of the Sea	100%	I	NB 3/5/07
3/6/07	Number the Stars	100%	I	NB 3-6-07
3/7/07	The Grey King	90%	I	NB 3-7-07
3/9/07	The higher power of lucky	100%	I	NB 3-9-07
3/8/07	The 21 balloons	100%	I	NB 3-8-07
3/19/07	Walk two Moons	90%	I	NB 3/19/07
3/19/07	Whipping Boy	90%	I	NB 3/19/07
3/22/07	Sarah Plain And Tall	100%	I	NB 3-22-07

For a blank Newbery Book Club Log template, see page 134.

 From *For the Love of Reading: Guide to K–8 Reading Promotions* by Nancy L. Baumann. Santa Barbara, CA: Libraries Unlimited. Copyright © 2013.

 **Notes**

CHAPTER 5

Some of your books aren't the ones you want but you can get some ones you do want at Book Swap.

—Alayna, fourth grade

PURPOSE

To provide a venue for students to recycle reading material, build personal libraries, and promote recreational reading.

GOALS

To provide an activity for students to recycle gently read reading materials.

To provide an opportunity for readers to acquire "new" reading materials without cost.

To provide a literacy event to promote summer recreational reading.

MATERIALS

Promotional flyers advertising Book Swap

Boxes to store books acquired for the Book Swap

Gentle cleaning solution

Paper towels or rags

Goo Gone

Blank labels

Gum erasers

Magic Tape by 3M

Lysol spray

Shopping bags (plastic or paper)

Implementation of Book Swap

Preparation for Book Swap

Allow one month to prepare for Book Swap. For an end-of-the-year Book Swap in mid-May, begin the second week in April to promote Book Swap in classes, faculty meetings, with posters, flyers, and a slide show presentation. Flyers are distributed two weeks prior to the swap. One fourth of 8 × 11 copy paper makes the perfect reminder and reduces paper. Student-made posters for hallways and an article in the PTA newsletter for April and May about Book Swap (see newsletter) create interest and motivation. This builds excitement and helps students decide which books to donate to Book Swap. The announcement in the PTA newsletter provides information to families on the operation of the Book Swap. Use morning announcements to promote Book Swap with a daily countdown. Visit student council in April to discuss Book Swap with student representatives. Student council is an excellent resource for student volunteers and promoting Book Swap. Attend PTA meetings and provide a presentation similar to the slide show given to students. Parents, caregivers, teachers, and the principal appreciate being informed of this activity.

So many good books to choose from at Book Swap.

Good promotion yields good results, so begin early. Line up several parent volunteers to help you take in books. Have a Book Swap orientation with volunteers so that they understand which books can be accepted. Include a list of swap guidelines for accepting donations. Purchase a gentle cleaner to wipe off covers, labels to cover inscriptions, and Goo Gone to gently remove labels and other sticky stuff. Gum erasers can remove pencil marks. Lysol spray helps disinfect the books and make them smell fresh. Have rags and paper towels available. Once the books are refreshed, store them in boxes. Label boxes with Fic, E, NF, and ER. Books can be sorted by category as they are readied. This makes it easier for setup. Collect plastic shopping bags from grocery stores or use leftover ones from book fairs. Students can also bring in reusable grocery shopping bags.

Book display is important. Creating a fun and festive atmosphere is essential in promoting Book Swap. If it occurs at the end of the year, wear summery hats and festive summer attire such as Hawaiian shirts, flip-flops, and leis. Play summertime music such as *The Beach Boys*. Use flamingo string lights and flamingo yard displays to create interest. Plastic tablecloths and brightly colored fabric remnants are useful for creating attractive displays. Scholastic's Book Fair website has numerous ideas for themes and book displays. Setting up Book Swap like a book fair delights students as no money is exchanged which is part of the fun and excitement. Everyone loves a good bargain!

Book Swap Guidelines for Donations

✦ Gently read titles—no writing, coloring, yellowed pages, and rips.

✦ The swap test: "Would you swap for this book?" (based on its condition).

✦ Must look almost new, like it only has been read several times.

✦ Check with parents or caregivers to be sure it is okay to swap this book. No family heirlooms or treasures.

✦ No adult or teen titles (for elementary swaps). Be selective in accepting "tween titles."

✦ No magazines or religious titles, manuals, and "restaurant or cereal titles."

✦ Must be appropriate for elementary students (for elementary swaps)

✦ 10 tickets will be given for 10 quality books. Additional books are viewed as a donation to the Book Swap.

Book Swap at Middle School

Similar procedures apply for a successful swap at middle school. Planning, publicity, and presentation are the components for hosting a successful event. The acceptable book guidelines will change as tween, teen, and appropriate adult titles are necessary. Series books are highly popular. Take in elementary titles if they are of high interest but easy reading level, for example, Goosebumps or nonfiction. Serving light snacks and drinks is well received by teens. Creative book displays, music, and ambience are important and shows respect for your clientele. The student council or library advisory group can assist with book donations, publicity, and running the swap.

Additional Tips

Keep set times to accept books. Before school, at lunch, and after school are good times to accept Book Swap titles. Students receive a ticket for each accepted title up to 10 tickets.

Encourage students to "try out" the Book Swap by swapping one book. This encourages more students to participate.

Have students write their initials and homeroom code on the back of the tickets.

Teachers can hold tickets until the swap or students should keep them at home until the Book Swap.

Keep a running list of names of students, homeroom, date, and number of tickets given. This helps provide a list if a student forgets or loses his or her tickets. In addition, this list provides names for teachers to release students to the swap. The list is used to admit students to the swap and also those who missed the swap. Last of all, this list provides statistics for your records.

Preplanning for Book Swap

Check the school calendar and secure a date for the Book Swap. Request the school secretary or the principal to place the Book Swap on the master school calendar.

Step-By-Step for book swap

One Month Out

◆ Design the Book Swap flyer. Copy on brightly colored copy paper. Cut and store flyers until distribution time.

◆ Design Book Swap tickets. Copy on bright colored copy paper. Cut and store until books are brought in for the swap.

◆ Write several promotional articles for school-wide morning announcements and school website.

- ✦ Schedule a student council visit to present Book Swap to room representatives.

- ✦ Contact the PTA secretary and request being placed on the agenda.

- ✦ Write an article for the PTA newsletter and send it to the newsletter chairperson.

- ✦ Create a slide show to promote the Book Swap with parents and students.

- ✦ Gather boxes to store Book Swap donations in until the event.

Three Weeks Out

- ✦ Make Book Swap posters and hang them throughout school. Student council or art classes can create posters.

- ✦ Attend student council meeting and present Book Swap to representatives. This is a good time to request volunteers.

- ✦ Attend PTA meeting and present Book Swap to parents and caregivers. This is a good time to ask for volunteers.

- ✦ Place Book Swap announcement on school or library website.

- ✦ Purchase Goo Gone, Lysol spray, labels, gum erasers, and paper towels for book refreshing.

Two Weeks Out

- ✦ Present Book Swap to classes during class visits.

- ✦ Read Book Swap announcement daily before school and at dismissal.

- ✦ Place Book Swap flyers in teachers' mailboxes for distribution.

- ✦ Hold two volunteer sessions, one for adults and one for students.

- ✦ Take in books from students for the swap.

- ✦ Refresh books that have been donated.

- ✦ Purchase fabric remnants and plastic tablecloths for book display.

- ✦ Purchase or borrow straw hats or beach hats, plastic flamingos, Beach Boys/ beach music, and any other decorative items.

One Week Out

- ✦ Continue accepting and refreshing book donations.

- ✦ Continue announcements in the morning and at dismissal time.

- ✦ Have music ready.

Day Before

✦ Last announcement for Book Swap. Books will be accepted *before* school on the day of the Book Swap.

✦ Send a list of participating students and time of Book Swap to classroom teachers.

Day of Book Swap

✦ Accept the last book donations *before* school. Refresh the books and add them to donations.

✦ Set up book displays. Use signs for fiction (Fic), easy (E), nonfiction (NF), and picture books.

✦ Set out customer bags for books on the checkout table.

✦ Make several copies of Book Swap participation list. Tape to checkout table.

✦ Use a recycling box for used Book Swap tickets.

✦ Play CDs and put on "summery clothing."

Easy level books for swapping.

Beginning chapter books to select.

Nonfiction books.

During the Book Swap

✦ Assign two volunteers to check out participants. One volunteer crosses off names and takes tickets, while the other volunteer puts books in shopping bags.

✦ Assign several volunteers to straighten book displays and put out additional books. They can assist with helping students find books they may want.

✦ Make sure all participants attend the Book Swap. Find out if anyone is absent. Make a note to include absent students when they return to school.

✦ Assign a volunteer to take photographs of the event.

Many great fiction selections for swapping.

It's a hard decision!

Hmm, this looks good!

After the Book Swap

✦ Take down the displays and box up the leftover books.

✦ Put all the tables and chairs back in the original position.

✦ Assign student volunteers to remove all posters.

✦ Take leftover books to the public library for their book sale.

✦ Write a report to include number of participants, volunteers, and donated books.

✦ Write thank you notes to all volunteers.

Book Swap June 3, 2009

Name	Number of Tickets	Teacher
Jennifer Aaland	10	2W
Preston K.	2	2W
Alex C.	2	2W
Gabby B.	2	4W
Brooke W.	2	2W
Dawson	10	5H
Sarah Argyle	10	3P
Cathryn L.	10	3B
Daniel	2	2E
Allison	3	2H
Mark A.	10	1H
Brienna G.	6	2E
Emily Z.	1	2E
Rachael	5	2E
Colin R.	9	5O
Jacob P.	1	2H
Holly W.	6	3P
Isaac	8	3B
Lizzie	1	5O
Jacob G.	4	6M
Ethan B.	3	5H
Kristian	2	3P
Michael W.	5	6C
Katie W.	6	3P

From *For the Love of Reading: Guide to K–8 Reading Promotions* by Nancy L. Baumann. Santa Barbara, CA: Libraries Unlimited. Copyright © 2013.

(Your number) Annual Book Swap!
When: (Your date)
Where: (Your school name)

Swap your good used books for some new titles. Only books in GREAT condition will be accepted—no torn pages or covers, no writing or coloring inside, no bent or yellowed pages, no Golden Books or religious titles. Receive 1 ticket per book—maximum of 10 tickets allowed. You may bring in more than 10 books, but you will still receive 10 tickets for swapping. **Bring in your "gently read" books to the library from (your dates).** This is a terrific chance to get some "new" books.

Bring in Books that You Would Want to Receive in the Swap

Questions: Call (your name and contact number)

E-mail: (Your e-mail address)

 From *For the Love of Reading: Guide to K–8 Reading Promotions* by Nancy L. Baumann. Santa Barbara, CA: Libraries Unlimited. Copyright © 2013.

REDEEM FOR 1 BOOK

(Your School) Book Swap

(Your Date)

Redeem for 1 book

Redeem for 1 book

(Your School) Book Swap

(Your Date)

Redeem for 1 book

REDEEM FOR 1 BOOK

(Your School) Book Swap

(Your Date)

Redeem for 1 book

REDEEM FOR 1 BOOK

(Your School) Book Swap

(Your Date)

REDEEM FOR 1 BOOK

REDEEM FOR 1 BOOK

(Your School) Book Swap

(Your Date)

REDEEM FOR 1 BOOK

REDEEM FOR 1 BOOK

(Your School) Book Swap

(Your Date)

REDEEM FOR 1 BOOK

REDEEM FOR 1 BOOK

(Your School) Book Swap

(Your Date)

REDEEM FOR 1 BOOK

REDEEM FOR 1 BOOK

(Your School) Book Swap

(Your Date)

REDEEM FOR 1 BOOK

REDEEM FOR 1 BOOK

(Your School) Book Swap

(Your Date)

Redeem for 1 book

Redeem for 1 book

(Your School) Book Swap

(Your Date)

Redeem for 1 book

REDEEM FOR 1 BOOK

(Your School) Book Swap

(Your Date)

REDEEM FOR 1 BOOK

REDEEM FOR 1 BOOK

(Your School) Book Swap

(Your Date)

REDEEM FOR 1 BOOK

REDEEM FOR 1 BOOK

(Your School) Book Swap

(Your Date)

REDEEM FOR 1 BOOK

REDEEM FOR 1 BOOK

(Your School) Book Swap

(Your Date)

REDEEM FOR 1 BOOK

Notes

CHAPTER 6

One Book One School
Community Read

You ARE having a One Book, One School Event next year, right?
—Parent of a third-grade student

I never knew that sharing a book nightly with my children and attending the discussion would be so much fun.
—Parent of a kindergarten and a second-grade student

PURPOSE

To promote recreational reading and involve the entire school community in a literacy project through reading and discussing high-quality children's and young adult literature.

GOALS

To involve students, families, and school faculty in a high-level discussion focusing on literary elements as prescribed by Common Core State Standards and AASL Standards for 21st-Century Learners.

To bring families to school for a literacy event.

To promote daily reading at home.

To involve community members in discussion groups as facilitators or group members.

To experience the thrill of being part of a literary community through reading the same book.

MATERIALS AND SUPPLIES

Paperback copies of the selected novel for everyone

Trivia questions, weekly guiding questions, and discussion prompts

Slide presentation of the selected novel(s) for the school-wide assembly

Raffle prizes for trivia contests

Door prizes for One Book One School (OBOS) family night

Dinner for OBOS night participants

Character costume

Implementation of One Book One School

Preparation for One Book One School

Long-range planning and a dedicated committee are the keys to a successful One Book One School (OBOS) event. Begin at the end of the school year or the first PTA and faculty meeting of the new school year. Explain the goals and objectives of this project and request a committee to assist in planning the event from the faculty and parents or PTA. Meet the following week to begin planning for OBOS. Items for discussion are a date for OBOS family night, time, book, kickoff assembly, dinner, group facilitators, weekly trivia and guide questions, discussion group prompts, trivia and door prizes, and community service project.

Kickoff Assembly

Once a date for OBOS night has been selected, begin planning the kickoff assembly. Check the school calendar for a 30-minute block for an all-school assembly. Invite your principal, fellow teachers, parents, public librarian, or community member(s) to assist you in enthusiastically promoting the event. Prepare an informative and lively slideshow to include a book talk, author information, and procedures so that everyone is excited. A skit and/or a reader's theater of a scene from the book will be well-received by the student body. Make students feel as though they can't wait to get their hands on the book and begin reading. Distribute the books and book schedule with guided reading questions when students return to the classroom. Begin OBOS reading that evening!

Book Selection

Discuss a possible book or books to be read for OBOS at the first committee meeting. Some schools opt for two different books being read and discussed, for example, one book for K-2 and a second title for Grades 3–5. This allows for a greater choice of titles to interest both age groups. Titles should be carefully selected for quality and appeal for a diverse group of readers. Additionally, the title should be available in paperback as it is less expensive. Consult John Newbery Medal lists, School Library Journal Best Books Lists, International Reading Association (IRA) Children's or Young Adult Choices, Jim Trelease's Read-Aloud Handbook, and American Library Association's (ALA's) Recommended Print/Media List to begin the selection process. Several literacy groups, such as "Read to Them" and "Share Our Books," organize and promote OBOS events. They provide annotated lists of books that have proven to be "winners." Both groups have websites explaining benefits of an OBOS read and provide a manual for organizing an event. "Share Our Book" provides 250–300 book sets in various titles to borrow free of charge for 6 weeks. The books are donated by authors and publishers. They provide a welcoming video, teacher's guide, and trivia questions. When the project is completed, the school packs up the books and ships them to the next school on the list. "Read to Them" provides a manual, book suggestions, and more. This organization assists in planning the entire event from a sample letter to parents, book selection, and extension activities. Schools around the United States participating in the OBOS program are highlighted and provide many good ideas. While "Read to Them" has a membership fee, it saves time and money especially if this is your first OBOS event or have a small committee. If you are doing it yourself, create a list of selections and assign committee members to read two or three of the books. At the next meeting, vote on the title or titles to be used. If purchasing the books, contact a vendor. Seek funding for the book purchase from PTA, principal's fund, family donations, and grants.

Read on if you are going to plan an OBOS event on your own. If you are going to use "Read to Them" or "Share Our Books" programs, you can follow their manuals for planning.

Weekly Reading, Guided Questions, Trivia Questions and Group Discussion Prompts, and Skype Author Visits

Once your book decision is made, begin creating the questions, prompts, and trivia questions. Check publisher or author websites for discussion questions, book summaries, book trailers, Skype author opportunities, and extension activities. Create a reading schedule on a bookmark with guided questions for families to discuss as they read. Include vocabulary words and background information that will be helpful to the reader and listeners. Announce daily trivia questions during morning announcements. Have classrooms complete trivia questions and return answers to the office. Holding the trivia contests within the classroom promotes book discussion and increases interest in family night. An OBOS committee member checks the answers and places correct entries in a drawing box. A drawing is held the next morning during announcements. Post the reading schedule and guided reading questions on the school's website. Skype author visits may be an option. Check the publisher's website for authors that host Skype author visits.

Community Members and Volunteers

Solicit community volunteers to assist as discussion leaders or members. If you have a university or community college, contact the education department. Future teachers and their professors may participate as part of a class assignment or service project. Student groups such as the National Education Association for education majors can be contacted to participate. Sororities, fraternities, and ROTC may be interested in participating as a service project. High-school clubs are a good source for volunteers. Use them as discussion group members and assisting with registration and dinner. Performing a skit for the evening's program and running a trivia contest about the book during dinner are additional tasks for volunteers. Invite the youth librarians from the public library to collaborate on this event. School librarians can reciprocate by participating during Summer Reading Club events. Prepare volunteers as to what their jobs entail during the event. Good communication and training with volunteers is essential.

University of Wyoming Children's Literature students and their professor participate in OBOS Family Night.

Community Awareness and Social Responsibility

Include a community service activity as part of OBOS read. This teaches students the importance of giving back to their community. For example, as part of the programming for *A Dog's Life*, a spokesperson from the local humane society spoke to students about the responsibility of owning a pet. *A Dog's Life* involves strays and pets who are "dumped" after their owners don't want them anymore. With student council's help, a dog, cat, and small pet supply drive ran during the month of OBOS reading and literacy night. A large amount of greatly needed supplies and donations were collected and presented to the humane society.

Results

The response for this activity was extremely positive. Most schools host a "family night" during the school year. OBOS is a meaningful way to encourage parents and caregivers to attend a school event and involve the entire school community.

✦ All students heard the book, *A Dog's Life*. Families and teachers read to students.

✦ Trivia contests were a big hit with students. Even adults wanted in on the trivia contests.

✦ The University of Wyoming children's literature class (spring semester) participated in OBOS as part of their classwork. Students and their professor attended the school event and participated or led discussion groups.

✦ Entire families attended the dinner and group discussion. Extended family members such as grandparents, relatives, and several nannies escorted students.

✦ For the first time event, 67 children and adults attended.

✦ Scholastic loaned a Clifford the Big Red Dog costume for greeting attendees.

✦ Wal-Mart donated stuffed animal dogs and raffle items.

✦ Domino's Pizza provided bread sticks, pizzas, drinks, and paper products at a reduced rate.

✦ The exit survey revealed that everyone wanted to have an OBOS event next year, and many surveyed said they would volunteer at such an event. Many attendees offered to donate for the book or dinner and to raise money for hosting a future OBOS.

✦ A sizable donation of kibble, treats, toys, blankets, and cash was collected for the humane society.

Everyone in the family is invited to OBOS Family Night.

"Hangin' Out" with Clifford at OBOS Family Night.

This planning schedule is for an OBOS event held in February or March.

Preplanning: End of the School Year or Beginning of New School Year (May/ June or August)

✦ Meet with school faculty and PTA to explain family literacy event—OBOS.

✦ Organize OBOS committee and set initial meeting.

✦ Contact your local university, sororities/fraternities, service clubs at the high school, or senior citizens groups for volunteers. University volunteers must be contacted early for the children's or young adult literature classes to place the event on their syllabus for second semester.

August/September

✦ Meet with OBOS committee. Agenda consists of setting a date for OBOS night and reading dates, kickoff assembly, book selection, choice of using an organization to assist in planning ("Read to Them" and "Share Our Books") or doing it yourself.

✦ Additional agenda items are volunteers; dinner planning; raffle items; guided reading; trivia questions; and discussion prompts; and Skype author interview.

October

✦ Meet with OBOS committee. Agenda consists of using "Read to Them" or "Share Our Books." The advantage of using "Read to Them" is savings on books, organizational manual and tips, and reliable advice on book selections for the event. But there is a membership fee. The advantage of using "Share Our Books" is nominal cost for using their books and organizational manual with tips. However, dates for available books may not fit in your schedule. Check the website for available dates and reservation information. Also the number of available titles is limited. Last of all, you can do it yourself. If you are experienced in running large events, OBOS will not be difficult especially with a competent committee.

If you are using "Read to Them" or "Share Our Books," follow their manuals. Doing it yourself? Read on!

Agenda for "Do-It-Yourself" OBOS Committee

November/December

All Committee	Publicity and Kickoff Assembly	Volunteers	Discussion, Prompts, and Trivia	Greet and Eat Committee
Order book, and obtain copy and read selection by next meeting	Design article for school newsletter and website	Solicit volunteers from high school or university groups	Check websites for discussion questions and create a reader's theater for assembly and family night	Plan menu and evening's schedule
Plan to participate in kickoff skit and reader's theater	Share event with local newspaper and see if they will cover event	Schedule meetings to discuss tasks with volunteers	Plan OBOS reading schedule and create bookmark (Microsoft Publisher)	Check with food vendors
Create an exit survey for participants	Create OBOS morning announcements		Plan trivia questions and discussion prompts	Prepare name tags for family night
	Plan assembly schedule, slideshow, skit, and book talk		Obtain trivia and door prizes	Obtain character costume

January: Four Weeks Out

All Committee	Publicity and Kickoff Assembly	Volunteers	Discussion, Prompts, and Trivia	Greet and Eat Committee
Make sure everyone has read the book	Design article for school newsletter and website, and send to newsletter editor and school tech person	Secure volunteers for discussion groups and greet and eat help	Create and practice reader's theater	Report on dinner menu and cost, prepare evening schedule
Check if all books have arrived and place recognition label inside	Ask local newspaper to send reporter to participate in event, also send a book to the reporter	Set two dates to discuss tasks with volunteers and e-mail reminders to volunteers	Create reading schedule and guided question bookmarks, which the committee previews	Secure character costume and the volunteer to wear it
Review exit survey, book trivia questions, guide questions, and discussion prompts	Create OBOS morning announcements and read to committee for any changes	Give discussion prompts to group facilitators three weeks prior to OBOS night	Prepare trivia questions and group discussion prompts, which the committee previews	Create name tags and divide discussion groups using related icon from book
	Plan assembly schedule, and preview skit, reader's theater, and slideshow		Secure trivia and door prizes	

One to Two Weeks Out

All Committee	Publicity and Kickoff Assembly	Volunteers	Discussion, Prompts, and Trivia	Greet and Eat Committee
Distribute books with guided question bookmark #1 to classrooms	Place large OBOS poster in entry	Hold last meeting with volunteers	Prepare and distribute guided question bookmarks, trivia questions, and OBOS discussion prompts	Receive RSVP slips and tally number of participants for food
Present kickoff assembly, and practice skit and reader's theater	Place OBOS announcement on outside marquee	E-mail volunteers any final instructions three days prior to event	Secure trivia and door prizes, and create door-prize tickets	Place order three days prior to event, also order some extras
Keep camera ready to document event	Send OBOS flyer home with students (same as announcement in newsletter and on website)			Prepare name tags as RSVPs are returned
Create receiving area for service project donations	Give OBOS morning announcements and trivia questions to announcer			Keep character costume ready

Week One of OBOS (*We Began on Friday)

✦ Morning announcements with OBOS spot.

✦ Kickoff assembly for OBOS; document the assembly with photographs and video.

✦ Pass out books to students in classrooms. Students should write their names on the book.

✦ Students take books home and begin reading with families/caregivers.

✦ Place a trivia response form in each teacher's mailbox on Friday evening.

✦ Each day, several new trivia questions are announced.

✦ Classes discuss answers and place them on trivia entry form. Student council representatives bring entry form to office on Friday morning.

✦ Answers are checked and winning classrooms announced at the end of the day.

✦ Distribute Week II guided question/reading schedule to classrooms on the next Friday.

✦ Student council representatives bring service project items to office.

Week Two of OBOS (*Thursday Evening Is OBOS Night)

✦ Morning announcements with daily OBOS spot and trivia questions and raffle Monday through Wednesday.

✦ Student council representatives bring donations to the office.

✦ Collect and tally OBOS night attendance all week. Finalize attendance on Tuesday with food vendor.

✦ Contact all volunteers on Tuesday with e-mail reminder of Thursday's event.

✦ On Thursday morning, place attendees in discussion groups. Make name tags with discussion group icon on name tag.

Clifford, the Big Red Dog, meets and greets friends.

OBOS Evening Schedule

5:30—All volunteers and organizers arrive at school. Set up welcoming table with name tags. Have door prize tickets ready to complete. Have a person wearing character costume dresses ready. Label rooms with discussion group names. Photographer is ready to document the evening.

6:00–6:15—Families arrive at school, sign in, pick up name tag, and fill in door prize entry form. View service project donations.

6:15–6:45—Dinner, announcements, door prize drawing, and gather with group leader to move to classroom for discussion.

A discussion group at OBOS Family Night.

6:45–7:15—Book discussion, reader's theater scene. Families complete a brief survey about the event. Group facilitators collect surveys and deliver to an OBOS committee member.

7:15—Dismiss for the evening.

7:15–7:30—Volunteers clean up cafeteria and welcoming table.

Friday—Deliver donated items.

OBOS Committee Recap Meeting (March/April)

Committee meets to evaluate the event and surveys. Make brief plans for next year's OBOS event. Write thank you notes to volunteers and donors. Include a photograph from the event. Create a bulletin board highlighting OBOS night.

Sample Items and Photos of OBOS Event with A Dog's Life by Ann Martin

Important Websites

For ideas about hosting an OBOS event, see

http://readtothem.org/

http://www.shareourbooks.org/

Lesson Plans, Writing Activities, Discussion Guide, and Vocabulary for A Dog's Life

"Squirrel" and "Bone" from A Dog's Life by Ann M. Martin are guests at OBOS Family Night.

http://www.scholastic.com/browse/video.jsp?pID=1640149541&bcpid=1640149541&bclid=1704115771&bctid=10026752001%E2%80%9D—Ann Martin reads from A Dog's Life

http://www.scholastic.com/teachers/lesson-plan/dog39s-life-teaching-guide

Library Website with OBOS Event

http://young.ipsd.org/Subpage.aspx?id=969

Vendors for Paperback Books

Scholastic—http://www.scholastic.com/teachers/

Sharing thoughts about the book *A Dog's Life* by Ann M. Martin.

Follett—http://www.follett.com/

Mackin—http://www.mackin.com/corp/index.html

Barnes and Noble—http://www.barnesandnoble.com

Your local independent book store

Publisher Sites with Discussion Guides

HarperCollins—http://www.harpercollinschildrens.com/Teachers/TeachingResources.aspx (look at Authors & Illustrators tab and Teaching Resources tab)

Random House—http://www.randomhouse.com/teachers/resources/ (author information, discussion guides, book talks, and common core tie-ins)

Penguin Young Readers—http://www.us.penguingroup.com/static/pages/youngreaders/teachers-librarians/tl-guides.html (teachers guides and activity kits, common core lesson plans, and author appearance information)

Simon & Schuster—http://teach.simonandschuster.net/Plan-an-Author-Appearance/How-To (planning for an author visit)

Simon & Schuster—http://search.simonandschuster.net/books/Category-Children-s-Fiction/_/N-fn4Zm2sm (children's fiction books with reading group guides)

Macmillan—http://us.macmillan.com/MacmillanSite/categories/Childrens/Guides/TeachersGuide (Discussion Guides, Reading Group Guides, and Teachers Guide)

Houghton Mifflin Harcourt—http://hmhtrade.com/bookclubs/teachers-resources-2/ (Discussion Guides and Teacher's Resources)

Peachtree Publishers—http://peachtree-online.com/index.php/resources/teachers-guides.html (Teacher Resources and Guides, in-person or virtual author visit)

Scholastic—http://www.scholastic.com/teachers/ (author interviews, and teacher's guides and activities)

Little Brown—http://littlebrownlibrary.com/category/resources/educator-guides/ (Educator Guides for Middle Grades, Picture Books, Young Adult)

Candlewick—http://www.candlewick.com/authill.asp?b=Author&aud=99&audss=11&pg=&m=actlist&a=&id=0&pix=n&audssmenu=0000 (Discussion and Teacher's Guides, Costume Requests)

School Library Journal—http://www.schoollibraryjournal.com/article/CA6673572.html, "Met Any Good Authors Lately? Classroom author visits can happen via Skype (here's a list of those who do it for free)"

Trivia Prizes

Decide how many classrooms will win the trivia contests and plan from that number.

Small Notepads, Decorative Pencils, and Erasers

Geddes—http://www.raymondgeddes.com

Oriental Trading—http://www.orientaltrading.com

Dollar General—http://www.dollargeneral.com

Door Prizes

✦ Small beanie baby-size stuffed animals

✦ Copies of a sequel of the book just read

✦ Copies of books by that author

✦ Copies of fiction and nonfiction books on the subject of the OBOS selection

Tip: A small stuffed animal and a book makes a nice door prize. For the children who didn't win a door prize, give away items from the trivia contests (small notepads, decorative pencils, and erasers). Then everyone goes home with a memory.

A Dog's Life

Questions to think about as you read

Parts III & IV

Dr. Roth, the vet was very kind to Squirrel. What kind things did Squirrel notice?

Explain why Rachel would have been a better owner than the Beckers.

Would Dr. Roth have allowed the Beckers to adopt Squirrel if she had known that Squirrel would have turned out to be a "summer dog"?

What did Squirrel mean when she thought that pet dogs were never lonely?

Talk about why Squirrel didn't allow Jean and Hal to know about her.

How did Squirrel's life change as she became an old dog?

Talk about why Squirrel was hesitant to go into Susan's house.

Discuss how Squirrel feels living with Susan.

Don't forget to send in your R.S.V.P. for OBOS Family Night!!

 From *For the Love of Reading: Guide to K–8 Reading Promotions* by Nancy L. Baumann. Santa Barbara, CA: Libraries Unlimited. Copyright © 2013.

One Book One School Community Read

Families are invited to read *A Dog's Life: Autobiography of a Stray* by Ann Martin. Reading will take place from January 28 (Week 1) to February 4 (Week 2). Over two weeks, families will read together and discuss the book at home. **A school-wide discussion will be held on Thursday, February 11, from 6:00 to 7:30 P.M.** University of Wyoming Education students and IPES faculty will lead group discussions. Dinner will be served and door prizes will be provided. The featured book, *A Dog's Life*, will be provided to every IPES family and faculty. Donations to offset the cost of the book will be accepted. Please send a check to IPES PTA or cash to Janie in the office. Check out this website, which has activities for the book: http://www.scholastic.com/dogslife. It also includes games and information about *A Dog's Life*. A service project for the Laramie Humane Society will begin on February 1 to gather dog food, chew bones, toys, collars beds, and other dog supplies. Other pet items may be donated too, for example, for cats or rabbits. Please complete the R.S.V.P if you plan to attend the family book discussion and pizza night! Questions: contact Mrs. Baumann at nbaumann@acsd1.org or 721-4490.

• •

Clip off and return to your teacher!

One Book One School Community Read Discussion and Pizza Night

Yes, we will attend the family book discussion and pizza night!

Total number of persons _____

Student(s) names_____

Parent(s) & Adults names_____

Everyone in your family is welcome to attend!

Sample Name Tags for OBOS Family Night

Monique

Steve

Mary Jo

 From *For the Love of Reading: Guide to K–8 Reading Promotions* by Nancy L. Baumann. Santa Barbara, CA: Libraries Unlimited. Copyright © 2013.

Notes

CHAPTER 7

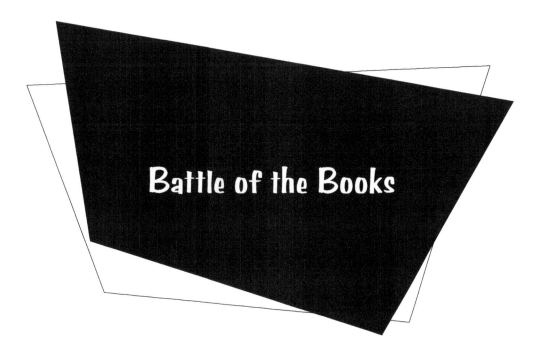

I participated in Battle of the Books because my sister said it was fun and I like to compete.

—Henry, fourth grade

I loved Battle of the Books, there were lots of good books, and I continued reading with some of the same authors.

—Katie, fourth grade

Yes, I participated because of all the fun I had doing Battle of the Books last year!

Gabby, fifth grade

PURPOSE

To promote recreational reading, teamwork, and academic excellence through reading high-quality children's and young adult literature.

GOALS

To build a recreational reading habit through reading of Battle of the Books titles.

To promote libraries and literature.

To promote teamwork.

To promote competition with an academic focus.

To promote collaboration by librarians, students, teachers, and administrators within a school and throughout the district.

To promote school spirit.

To promote community–school partnership.

MATERIALS

Sets of Battle of the Book titles

Battle of the Books slideshow and brochure

Reading record chart and stickers

Battle of the Books question sets and manual

Laminated signs "A" and "B" used in competition

Trophies from trophy store

Implementation of Battle of the Books

Preparation for Battle of the Books

Discuss the Battle of the Books program with stakeholders in your school or district. Discuss the purpose, goals, benefits, and cost of the program. Use Battle of the Books websites to explain the program and its benefits for students. If a neighboring school district or public library is hosting a program, attend a Battle of the Books competition and talk with the organizers.

Commercial Battle of the Books Programs

Several Battle of the Books programs are available for purchase. They include an organizational manual, levels of prepared questions, and book lists for different age or grade levels. The book lists include high-quality children's and young adult literature with Newbery winners and honor books, and nonfiction as well. One program customizes questions for State Award Reading Lists and provides additional practice questions. Both programs involve a nominal fee for the Battle of the Books package or membership. The framework and questions for the program are then taken care of so that each school or district can add their traditions or special activities to personalize their Battle of the Books program.

Books

The books are the most expensive part of this program. The books are in paperback format. Having a minimum of two sets is necessary to have enough available for readers. Vendors and independent bookstores will usually work to provide the lowest price especially if it is a bulk purchase and used for Battle of the Books. Check your public library for copies of some of the classic titles. The reading list is available a year in advance so that allows time to acquire titles from your library, garage sales, donations, and book fair funds or book club points. Also check with the public library for audiobooks as some of your students will want to use this format. Books can be used later for classroom literature groups.

Funding Battle of the Books

Present a slideshow for PTA to explain the program. Any funding they can provide is great. Offer to split the cost of the program with them and your principal. That way they are investing but are not committing a large portion of their budget. Grants, principal's funds, faculty lounge vending machine profits, and community groups are other possible funding sources. The UniWyo Credit Union in Laramie, Wyoming, provided funding for books, judges and timekeepers, and prize money for the winning teams. The Wyoming State Bank and Georgia Power company provided yearly support for the Battle of the Books questions and trophies. A donor recognition tag was placed on the trophies to acknowledge the donation. Marquees in town featured Battle of the Books competition dates. Invite donors to the district competition and recognize them or invite them to take part in the competition by presenting the trophies or acting as a judge. Barnes and Noble hosted a fund-raiser with a mock Battle of the Books night at the bookstore. Teams from schools "battled" in a round robin of mini-battles. A percentage of sales that month was placed into a Battle of the Books fund for participating schools. Barnes and Noble also provided a discount on book orders.

Battle of the Books volunteer judges from UniWyo Credit Union.

Mr. Slyman, principal, celebrates with the team captain at the Battle of the Books luncheon.

Cupcakes and pizza to celebrate Battle of the Books teams.

Having fun with Battle of the Books team.

Fun Tips

✦ Invite students to dress as a team, school T-shirts or all in one color shirt for competition.

✦ Bring a stuffed animal mascot to represent them.

✦ Honor teams with a luncheon with the principal after competition.

✦ Have students write thank you notes to donors.

✦ Include pictures of the teams along with thank you notes.

✦ Have students name their teams.

✦ Decorate a bulletin board with team members in a prominent location in the entryway of the school.

✦ Create a highly visible and striking Battle of the Books display.

✦ Prepare a slideshow to promote Battle of the Books to students. Use photos and videos of previous teams and competitions.

✦ Host "working lunches" in the library to practice before competition.

✦ Provide etiquette lessons on teamwork, inclusion, and sportsmanship with the school counselor.

✦ Host a catered luncheon in the library for Battle of the Books teams after competition. Show slides of teams and competition.

Results

✦ A majority of students in fifth and sixth grades participated in Battle of the Books.

✦ Cross grade-level teams worked together.

- Many students read more books during Battle of the Books season than any other time of the year.

- Students recruited other students to be on their team.

- Students participated because of the fun a sibling had on a Battle of the Books team.

- Teams created questions and practiced on their own, face to face or through social networking.

- The Battle of the Books program spread from initially 2 schools to 3 schools the next year, until all 14 schools in the district participated. Then it spread to middle schools as the students wanted to continue the program.

- The Battle of the Books program is 12 years old in Athens, Georgia. Several surrounding districts began their own competition after observing the Athens program. Battle of the Books was introduced in Laramie, Wyoming, in 2008 with one school and now includes all the elementary and the middle schools.

- Students surveyed said they liked the friendly competition against other schools, working on a team, and reading the books.

- Parents and caregivers enjoyed observing their children working toward a goal and the academic competition.

- Family support was provided through extra trips to the library and discussing the books at home.

- The UniWyo Credit Union judges and timekeepers requested to continue each year as volunteers in the program.

- A team consisting of mainly ESOL members won 2nd place out of 13 elementary schools. Teachers and volunteers coached the team throughout the Battle of the Books season.

Step-by-Step Planning for a Late February/March Battle of the Books

End of the School Year (May/June)

- Meet with stakeholders to discuss and go forward with Battle of the Books.

- Assemble a Battle of the Books committee.

- Review various Battle of the Books websites.

- Seek donations for manual, questions, books, and trophies.

- Seek and apply for grant funding.

- Purchase Battle of the Books program from the vendor.

Beginning of the School Year (August/September)

✦ Meet with PTA to present Battle of the Books and request support. Invite last year's teams to talk to PTA members about their experience with Battle of the Books. Stage a mock battle for PTA members.

✦ Acquire bids for books from vendors. Order books as early as possible.

✦ Work with participating schools to set dates for reading, school competitions, and district competition.

✦ Reserve auditorium at high school or public library for district competition.

✦ Check on bus transportation and "pool" bus rides with schools close to one another.

October

✦ Time to place book order from vendors.

November/December

✦ Meet with the Battle of the Books committee and participating schools to disseminate Battle of the Books manual, school competition questions, review dates for competitions.

✦ Review Battle of the Books procedures with adult coaches (librarians and teachers).

✦ Assign subcommittees for trophies, district competition, and volunteers.

✦ Create a Battle of the Books promotional slideshow for students.

✦ Books arrive, participants pick up at designated school.

✦ Process books if necessary.

January

✦ Present slideshow to introduce and promote Battle of the Books to students.

✦ Present students with Battle of the Books booklist on a bookmark (in Battle of the Books manual).

✦ Have books on display and ready for checkout.

✦ Post reading record chart for students to record which titles they have read (some schools use Accelerated Reader quizzes as a check on students reading).

✦ Copy and send home Battle of the Books brochure.

✦ Post Battle of the Books information on school website and in school newsletter.

✦ Students read books for the next three to four weeks.

Book List 2009
Grades 5 and 6

Black Storm Comin'—Wilson

Cryptid Hunters by Smith

Heat—Lupica

Jeremy Fink and the Meaning of Life—Mass

The Seven Professors of the Far North—Fardell

Rodzina—Cushman

Phineas L. MacGuire Erupts—Dowell

The Spy who Came in from the Sea—Nolan

The Twenty-One Balloons—Pene du Bois

For more information about Battle of the Books, contact Nancy Baumann, Indian Paintbrush Elementary 307-721-4490 nbaumann@acsd1.org

Battle of the Books 2009

Battle of the Books

Battle of the Books is a reading motivational program designed to improve reading comprehension. Students form teams of five, select a captain, divide up a reading list of 10 books, and read the books over several months. Teams meet in competition refereed by a questioner and a timer and answer a set number of questions, like "In which book does a character drink poisoned medicine meant for someone else?" The top scoring team is the school champion. Books selected are at a variety of reading levels and genres, Newbery Award winners, Honor books, and classics. Some of the titles are from authors with a large body of work in the hope that students will want to continue reading when the competition is completed.

Purpose of Battle of the Books

❖ Promotes recreational reading

❖ Promotes libraries and literature

❖ Promotes competition with an academic focus

❖ Promotes teamwork

❖ Promotes collaboration by librarians, students, teachers, and administrators within a school and throughout the district

❖ Promotes the importance of reading

❖ Promotes school spirit

Teams

A Battle of the Books team should have five members. Students form their own teams and select one member as team captain. It is the responsibility of the team captain to see that team members read all of the books. Some teams try to have all members read all of the books; others divide the books up with each team member being the "authority" on two books.

Competitions

Teams compete at school and district levels.

- School counselor and principal discuss sportsmanship, friendship, and teamwork with students.
- Arrange for media outlets to cover the Battle of the Books district competition.

February

- Students form teams after two weeks of reading. Some schools require students to read two to three books to be able to join a team to show intent of participating.
- Hold a callout for teams to "register" and receive a Battle of the Books schedule and a bookmark.
- Teams designate a team captain who receives Battle of the Books rules.
- Take team photos for bulletin board. Take one serious and one "funny" photo.
- Teams give themselves a name.
- Host "working lunches" in library to practice. BattleoftheBooks.com provides practice questions or students and coaches can write practice questions.
- The day before the school competition, meet with teams to discuss strategies and sportsmanship.

Serious at competition.

- Have school-level trophies ready to award.
- Battle of the Books volunteer judges and timekeepers meet to go over questions, rules, and timing.
- Conduct school competitions according to the Battle of the Books manual.
- Take photographs of all teams after competition.
- Set date for Battle of the Books luncheon for all teams.

District Competition

- Practice with school championship team the week before the contest.
- Students must have permission forms completed to attend competition.
- Review rules, strategies, and sportsmanship.
- Meet or e-mail with Battle of the Book committees to check on the status of all aspects of the district competition.

✦ The Battle of the Books manuals provide checklists for each level of competition.

✦ Document event with photographs and videos.

At Competition

✦ Escort students to auditorium. Teams sit together.

✦ Take photographs of all teams.

"Nerdy Princesses" celebrate at Battle of the Books luncheon.

After Competition

✦ Survey students and families about Battle of the Books program.

✦ Host luncheon in library for teams, principal, and coaches.

✦ Teams write thank you notes to donors and volunteers.

✦ Librarians write thank you notes to donors and volunteers.

✦ Battle of the Books committee meets to discuss program and procedures for next year.

Websites

Commercial Battle of the Books Programs

http://www.battleofthebooks.com/first.html

http://battleofthebooks.org/

Vendors

www.scholastic.com

www.barnesandnoble.com

www.mackin.com

www.follett.com

www.btol.com

Local independent bookstores

Book List
(year)
Grades (your grades)

Battle
Of the
Books
(year)

For More Information
about Battle of the
Books, contact
Put in your contact
information and logo

Battle of the Books

Battle of the Books is a reading motivational program designed to improve reading comprehension. Students form teams of five, select a captain, divide up a reading list of ten books, and read the books over several months. Teams meet in competition refereed by a questioner and a timer and answer a set number of questions like, "In which book does a character drink poisoned medicine meant for someone else?" The top scoring team is the school champion. Books selected are at a variety of reading levels and genres, Newbery Award Winners, Honor books, and classics. Some of the titles are from authors with a large body of work in the hope that students will want to continue reading when the competition is completed.

PURPOSE OF BATTLE OF THE BOOKS

❖ Promotes recreational reading

❖ Promotes libraries and literature

❖ Promotes competition with an academic focus

❖ Promotes teamwork

❖ Promotes collaboration by librarians, students, teachers, administrators within a school and throughout the district

❖ Promotes the importance of reading

Teams

A Battle of the Books team should have 5 members. Students form their own teams and select one member as team captain. It is the responsibility of the team captain to see that team members read all of the books. Some teams try to have all members read all of the books; others divide the books up with each team member being the "authority" on two books.

Competitions

Teams compete at school and district levels.

From *For the Love of Reading: Guide to K–8 Reading Promotions* by Nancy L. Baumann. Santa Barbara, CA: Libraries Unlimited. Copyright © 2013.

Notes

CHAPTER 8

Reading Millionaires Project

I never thought we'd be able to do it. But I am glad we did and it wasn't that hard.

—Claire, third grade

PURPOSE

To promote and build a recreational reading habit.

GOALS

To read 1,000,000 minutes or more during the school year.

To promote reading and create lifelong readers.

To improve vocabulary and comprehension.

To set and complete a long-term goal.

To involve the entire school community working toward a common goal.

To promote school spirit.

MATERIALS

Reading Teacher article: G. A. O'Masta and J. M. Wolf, "Encouraging Independent Reading through the Reading Millionaires Project," *The Reading Teacher* 44 (1991): 656–62

"Saving Books" weekly reading logs

Paperback books for weekly raffle

Pizza Hut Book-It Reading Program—http://www.bookitprogram.com/

6 Flags Read to Succeed Program—https://feedback.sixflags.com/rts/default.aspx

Incentives for reaching milestones: popcorn, cupcake, and pizza parties

"Mystery Readers" volunteers

School "Reading Millionaires" pennant

Implementation of Reading Millionaires

Preparation for Reading Millionaires

The Reading Millionaires' program involves the school faculty and families. Present the program to your administrator and governance committee. Discuss the mission, goals, faculty involvement, and cost. Next, discuss the program with the faculty and PTA parent group. Prepare a slide show to explain how Reading Millionaires will promote independent reading, build a reading habit, and involve families at a nominal cost. Discuss how the program will be run, for how long, and who will be involved. Reading Millionaires ran for 27 weeks at Barnett Shoals Elementary in Athens, Georgia. Prepare a Reading Millionaires brochure for faculty and for parents. Present the program at open house at the beginning of the school year.

Reading Millionaires Savings Book Reading Log

Prepare the Savings Book to go home every Thursday, for example. The first Savings Book describes the Reading Millionaires' program and includes a reading contract. One side features the Savings Book and the flip side has recommendations for books, apps, websites, reading tips, and school news. Light-colored green copy paper helps families recognize the Savings Book and ties in the money theme. The librarian or program coordinator creates logs and places copies in the teachers' mailboxes on

Wednesday. Enter the teacher's name in the teacher space prior to copying the logs. Teachers can assist by writing the child's name on the log or have students write their names when they are capable. Teachers place the Savings Books in the student's weekly folder that contains student work for the week and the class newsletter. Families take out the new log and place completed logs in the weekly folder to return to the teacher on Friday. During the week, students and families read and record minutes and materials they have read. Additional sheets may be added as needed. Savings Books are returned to the child's teacher and the minutes are entered on the online class Savings Book (see Pizza Hut Book-It's minute tracker). Completed Savings Books are filed in the student's cumulative folder. Each classroom's weekly total is e-mailed to the librarian who compiles the school's weekly minutes and adds the number to the previous week's total. The Reading Millionaires tally bulletin board is then updated with the new total of the week.

Reading Millionaires Rally

Kickoff Reading Millionaires with an all-school pep rally. Promoting the program with students and faculty creates a "buzz" of anticipation in being involved with a BIG event!! Invite your principal and librarian to introduce and explain what is in store for everyone. Have cheerleaders and mascots from your local high school and university to cheer on the students. Create a faculty cheerleading squad and have them cheer on students with some "reading" cheers. Lastly, have the school chorus perform a song or rap that involves reading. Send home the first Savings Book to begin reading after the rally.

Volunteers

Not all students will be read to or return Savings Books. Volunteer readers and listeners can listen to or read to students. Schedule Mystery Readers to read weekly in classrooms. Mystery Readers are community volunteers who are willing to read to several classrooms. Mystery Readers can be Wal-Mart, Target, and Starbucks employees; ROTC members; student athletes at high school and university levels; fraternity and sorority members; Junior League organizations; Rotary Clubs; fire fighters and police; and retirees. Provide Mystery Readers with books known to be *winners* to share with students. In addition, principals, counselors, paraprofessionals, librarians, cafeteria and custodial staff, and literacy coaches can be readers or listeners. Older students can act as reading buddies to younger students and earn reading minutes. Invite volunteers to participate in the Reading Millionaires assembly and a thank you brunch at the end of the year.

Results of the Reading Millionaires Program

Reading Millionaires was implemented in Athens, Georgia. Students reached 1,000,000 minutes and even read a little more for a grand total of 1,198,203 minutes. It was so well-received by the faculty and families that it was continued the following year. During the second year, the faculty recorded their reading in "Savings Books" like the students. Families and students were surveyed at the end of the year for comments about Reading Millionaires.

Reading Millionaires Results

✦ Students read 1,230,407 minutes in 1994 in 27 weeks and 1,280,699 minutes in 1995.

Reading Millionaires Bulletin Board.

Every student received a Reading Millionaires pennant.

✦ All students received a "Reading Millionaires" pennant funded by a mini-grant from the Clarke County School District, Athens, Georgia.

✦ In the first year, 9 students turned in a reading log **every** week, and 14 during the second year.

✦ 40 students were inducted in the "Reading Hall of Fame" for reading over 500 minutes in 1 week.

✦ 130 students earned 6 Flags Read to Succeed passes.

✦ 5 billboards in Athens highlighted the success of Reading Millionaires at Barnett Shoals Elementary.

✦ According to the family survey, bedtime was the most popular time for families to read together.

✦ Margery Mayer, president of Scholastic Education, provided a paperback book for every student to kickoff Reading Millionaires program.

Fun Tips

✦ Prepare a Reading Millionaires bulletin board, which changes weekly as the reading total increases. Also include 6 Flags Read to Succeed and Reading Hall of Fame recipients.

✦ Provide reading certificates and a book for "Perfect Readers" to students who have returned a Savings Book weekly and "All-Star Readers" for those who have returned logs 15 weeks or more.

✦ Have a "Reading Rap" or a "Reading Cheer" contest. Winners perform at the Reading Millionaires rally.

✦ Provide popcorn, cupcake, and pizza parties for classrooms as reading minute milestones are reached.

✦ Provide gift certificates for all students to purchase a book from the book fair. Scholastic book fairs have BOGO or 50% Off book fairs.

Six billboards around Athens, GA, celebrated our goal.

✦ Hold weekly raffles of paperback books for students who have turned in Savings Books.

✦ Be sure to digitally document all Reading Millionaires activities.

✦ I LIKE BIG BOOKS by Dowell Middle School on YouTube after School.

✦ Library Cheer—https://www.youtube.com/watch?v=jis3P6HFZ-M. Use Margaret Miles version

Step-by-Step Preparation for Reading Millionaires

Preplanning End of the School Year (May or June)

✦ Meet with administrators and school council to propose the Reading Millionaires program.

✦ Meet with faculty to discuss implementation of Reading Millionaires for the next school year.

✦ Meet with district technology staff to create a minute tracker similar to Pizza Hut's tracker or plan to utilize the Pizza Hut Book-It minute tracker.

- ✦ Solicit funding for Reading Millionaires pennants.
- ✦ Purchase paperback books for Reading Millionaires kickoff at the Scholastic BOGO or 50% Off book fair at the end of the school year.

School District Teacher Planning (August)

- ✦ Assemble a Reading Millionaires steering committee to coordinate pep rallies, volunteers, and publicity.
- ✦ Prepare a brief slide presentation and brochure for families and open house.
- ✦ Reading Millionaires steering committee plans rally and invites cheerleaders, mascots, and news sources.
- ✦ Include a request for reading volunteers in the PTA newsletter and school website.
- ✦ Copy Reading Millionaires logs per classroom enrollment. Light green copy paper calls attention to Reading Millionaires. Number the Savings Books, for example, Week 1, Week 2, etc.
- ✦ Schedule Reading Millionaire reading volunteer and Mystery Readers orientation.

First Week of School

- ✦ At faculty meeting, steering committee presents Reading Millionaires kickoff rally schedule.
- ✦ Technology department attends faculty meeting to demonstrate Reading Millionaires minute tracker.
- ✦ Post weekly Reading Millionaires news on the school website, school marquee, and in the school newsletter.

Second Week of School

- ✦ On Wednesday, place "Savings Books" in teacher's mailboxes.
- ✦ E-mail teachers reminders to pick up Savings Books 1 on Thursday morning.
- ✦ Hold Reading Millionaires kickoff rally on Thursday afternoon.
- ✦ Send Savings Books 1 home with students following rally.

Weeks 3–27

- ✦ Continue to prepare and deliver Savings Books.
- ✦ All class minutes are e-mailed to the librarian for tallying and updating the bulletin board.

◆ Morning announcements cite new reading totals and encourage students.

◆ Mystery Readers and volunteers continue to read to classes and students.

◆ Coordinate Pizza Hut Book-It and 6 Flags Read to Succeed programs with Reading Millionaires.

◆ Recognize students who have achieved Reading Hall of Fame, Perfect Reader, and All-Star Reader status on the Reading Millionaires bulletin board and morning announcements.

◆ Hold Savings Book raffle weekly for students turning in logs.

◆ Hold recognition events with a cupcake or popcorn party every time 250,000 reading minutes has been reached.

◆ Reading Millionaires steering committee evaluates accumulated minutes to make sure the goal will be reached by the completion date. Schedule D.E.A.R. events to accumulate additional minutes if needed.

◆ Steering committee plans end-of-the-year rally in February and invites cheerleaders, mascots, and guests.

◆ Order Reading Millionaires pennants in February.

One Month from the End-of-the-Year Rally

◆ Steering committee plans agenda for the end-of-the-year rally.

◆ Invitations to all volunteers for the rally-and-volunteer brunch are sent out.

◆ Hold a Reading Rap and a Reading Cheer contest for the rally.

Two Weeks from the End-of-the-Year Rally

◆ Keep cheering on and encouraging readers to accumulate minutes.

◆ Review the rally with the principal.

◆ Contact media for coverage of the rally.

◆ Send surveys to families.

◆ Sort pennants for classrooms.

◆ Create reading certificates for Perfect Readers and All-Star Readers.

◆ Select Reading Rap and Reading Cheer winners to perform at the rally.

One Week from the End-of-the-Year Rally

◆ Continue to record minutes through Week 27.

◆ Make a BIG announcement once 1,000,000 minutes is reached and continue to collect minutes through Week 27.

- ✦ E-mail reminders to all rally participants and media.
- ✦ Update the bulletin board with a large "We Did It!!" sign.
- ✦ Hold a practice for Reading Rap and Reading Cheer groups.

Day of Pep Rally

- ✦ Deliver Reading Millionaires pennants to classrooms to present to students after the rally.
- ✦ Principal welcomes students and commends their efforts.
- ✦ Steering committee introduces guests and cheerleaders.
- ✦ Student groups present "Reading Rap" and "Reading Cheer."
- ✦ Steering committee presents reading certificates to Perfect Readers and All-Star Readers.
- ✦ Guests, cheerleaders, and mascots present a cheer for students.
- ✦ Principal wraps up assembly!!

Reading Millionaires Wrap-up Activity

- ✦ Steering committee reviews family and faculty surveys.
- ✦ Steering committee reviews all Reading Millionaire activities to plan for next year.
- ✦ Steering committee writes thank you notes to volunteer readers.
- ✦ Steering committee shares a Reading Millionaires report with the principal, school council, PTA, and school board.

Websites

Pizza Hut Book-It—http://www.bookitprogram.com/

6 Flags Read to Succeed—https://feedback.sixflags.com/rts/default.aspx

Scholastic—www.scholastic.com

It's Elementary (pennants)—http://www.andersons.com/Elementary-School

Reading Songs—http://readingsongs.com/

I LIKE BIG BOOKS-Dowell M.S.—http://www.youtube.com/watch?v=tuZSfvHHMr4

Library Cheer—https://www.youtube.com/watch?v=jis3P6HFZ-M

Reading Cheers for Reading Millionaires Pep Rally

READ, READ, READ, READ, READ, READ, READ (say this while twisting at waist)
(Chant 3 times)
A MILLION MINUTES, A MILLION MINUTES
(Raise hands and shake them)

B-o-o-k-s
(Sing to the tune of BINGO)
We're a school that likes to read and books are what we read-OH
B-o-o-k-s, B-o-o-k-s, B-o-o-k-s, and Books are what we read-OH
(Sing 3 times)

We like reading, read every day-Hey Hey!
We like reading, OLE, OLE!!
We like reading-what did I say??
We like reading-OK OK!!

Who likes to read, I say the kids like to read (kids stand up)
And when the kids like to read, they read all day long!!
Who likes to read, I say the teachers like to read (teachers stand up)
And when the teachers like to read, they read all day long!!
Who likes to read, I say Mr. Clark likes to read (principal stands up)
And when Mr. Clark likes to read, he reads all day long!!
Who likes to read, I say "Hairy Dawg" likes to read (mascot stands up)
And when "Hairy Dawg" likes to read, he reads all day long!
Who likes to read, I say the "Lady Dawgs" like to read (student athletes stand up)
And when the "Lady Dawgs like to read, they read all day long!!
End chant with "Kids" like to read

Library Cheer

—Margaret Miles, California Library Conference, 2007

Library Cheer!
(Leader says what's in caps, crowd says what's in lower case)
Everybody says hip-hip-hooray!
L-I-B-R-A-R-Y
l-i-b-r-a-r-y
I SAID L-I-B-R-A-R-Y!
l-i-b-r-a-r-y
WHERE DO YOU GO FOR POETRY?
l-i-b-r-a-r-y
WHERE DO YOU GO FOR HISTORY?
l-i-b-r-a-r-y
WHERE DO YOU GO IF YOU'RE OLD AND SHY?
l-i-b-r-a-r-y
WHERE DO YOU GO TO LEARN HOW TO FLY?

l-i-b-r-a-r-y
I SAY LIBRARY, YOU SAY CARD
LIBRARY
card
LIBRARY
card
I GOT ONE, AND IT WASN'T TOO HARD
LIBRARY
card
LIBRARY
card
BIG BRICK BUILDING HOW SWEET IT LOOKS, SO TAKE ME IN TO THE LAND OF BOOKS
TO THE L-I-B-R-A-R-Y
l-i-b-r-a-r-y
IT'S BEEN IN YOUR TOWN FOR A HUNDRED YEARS, LET'S GIVE YOUR LIBRARY THREE BIG CHEERS!
Hip-Hip-Hooray! Hip-Hip-Hooray! Hip-Hip-Hooray!!

Reading Millionaires Club

Help your child save for his or her future by depositing reading minutes in the (Your School) Bank. Every time you help your child record the minutes spent reading, you help (Your School) get closer to its goal—to develop lifelong readers.

Regulations for Becoming a Member of the Reading Millionaires Club

1. Both parent/guardian and child must sign the contract.

2. The numbers of minutes spent reading can be deposited when one of the following conditions are met:

   ✦ Being read to by someone like mom, dad, or a relative.

   ✦ Reading aloud to someone.

   ✦ Reading silently.

3. The number of minutes spent in reading needs to be recorded in the Savings Book.

4. Keep the Savings Book in a folder or binder.

5. Any engagement in reading counts. Please record the titles if possible, because this will help your child appreciate and gain satisfaction from the reading he or she is doing. For example, a child might write in the Savings Book "Charlotte's Web." If the same book is read more than once or continues the next day, just record it again.

6. When reading is done with more than one child, each child records a deposit. Each Savings Book will be collected at the close of the week. A (Your School) Bank statement giving the school's balance will be published in the school newsletter and on the website at the end of the month.

7. Read as many days as you can for as long as the child maintains interest and enthusiasm. Never mind if you skip a day or two. KEEP IT FUN. DO WHATEVER WORKS FOR YOU!

Please clip and return the following contract to your child's teacher. We hope all (Your School) students join Reading Millionaires Club!

Contract

I wish to become a lifelong reader and deposit my reading minutes in (Your School) Reading Millionaires Bank.

Student's signature_____Parent/Guardian_____

BARNETT SHOALS READING MILLIONAIRE$ CLUB
$$$ Savings Book $$$

Name _____ Grade _____ Room _____

Week of _____

Day	No. of Minutes Read	Title of Reading Material
Fri.		
Sat.		
Sun.		
Mon.		
Tues.		
Wed.		
Thur.		
TOTAL		

_____
(Parent/Guardian Signature)

 From *For the Love of Reading: Guide to K–8 Reading Promotions* by Nancy L. Baumann. Santa Barbara, CA: Libraries Unlimited. Copyright © 2013.

THE BEST LEADING THE REST

Barnett Shoals Newsletter

BARNETT SHOALS ELEMENTARY SCHOOL - 3220 BARNETT SHOALS ROAD - ATHENS, GEORGIA 30605 - 706 / 357- 5334

VOLUME 2, NO. 9   MAY, 1994

WE DID IT!

OVER

1,000,000 MINUTES

The students and families at Barnett Shoals School have done it! We have read 1,000,000 minutes. Actually we have read 1,198,203 minutes as of May 11, 1994. The students read many kinds on interesting things from *Charlotte's Web, Totally Disgusting,* Bible stories and lessons, cereal boxes, Goosebump books, newspapers, *Sports Illustrated, Ranger Rick, Highlights, Where the Red Fern Grows,* Jennifer Murdley's *Toad* and many other books, magazines, and *Nintendo* instructions. We are so PROUD of all of you--to all the families for helping read and complete Savings Books and to all the students for reading to yourself and others. Our hats are off to you!

The Reading Millionaire's Club was so successful that it will be conducted again next year. But next year all the faculty and staff at Barnett Shoals will also receive a Savings Book on Friday, and will be reading and saving minutes just like the students and their families. We are all dedicated at Barnett Shoals to creating lifelong readers. Again, congratulations to all the students and their families for reaching such a significant goal.

❖   ❖   ❖

The

Reading Millionaires

Project

"Our goal is to read 1,000,000 minutes"

Your school contact

information

Don't FORGET!

Help us reach our goal of reading 1,000,000 Minutes!

- Read nightly
- Record minutes read in the Savings Book
- Return Savings Book on (your day)
- Check school web site and newsletter for the new weekly tally of minutes read
- Have Fun

122   From *For the Love of Reading: Guide to K–8 Reading Promotions* by Nancy L. Baumann. Santa Barbara, CA: Libraries Unlimited. Copyright © 2013.

Tips for Reading Aloud Together

- Choose books that are interesting to your child.

- If your child asks a question, stop and answer his or her questions.

- Read with expression. Be a little dramatic!

- Discuss what might happen next or might happen to the characters after you finish the story.

- Read aloud together every day even if your child can read independently.

- Get a library card. Ask your librarian for suggestions.

What to Read

Weekly Savings Books will include tips and suggestions for reading. Here are some ideas for starting.

- Chapter & Picture Books

- Poetry & Nonfiction

- Magazines & Manuals

- Scout Manuals

- Newspapers

- Game Instructions & Cookbooks

- Comics & Graphic Novels

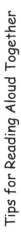

The goal of Reading Millionaires is to promote recreational reading and build a reading habit. Practicing reading makes students better readers. Earn reading minutes by reading to your child or together as a family. Each child that is read to earns reading minutes for his or her Savings Book. Start a chapter book with your family. Listen to your child read his or her favorite book. Turn off TV for 30 minutes and read together as a family. Your child also earns minutes by reading independently.

From *For the Love of Reading: Guide to K–8 Reading Promotions* by Nancy L. Baumann. Santa Barbara, CA: Libraries Unlimited. Copyright © 2013.

 **Notes**

CHAPTER 9

Additional Reading
Promotional Ideas

I participated because I love challenges and they are fantastic books.

—Hailey, fifth grade

I did it, and I did it because some of my friends promoted me to do it, and I really enjoyed it.

—Kyle, fifth grade

NEWBERY BOOK CLUB

PURPOSE

To encourage reading of John Newbery Medal Award titles and honor books.

To recognize readers for academically challenging themselves.

GOALS

To promote recreational reading.

To promote reading of award-winning literature.

To improve vocabulary and comprehension.

To set and complete a long-term goal.

MATERIALS

Newbery Award and Honor titles

Slide presentation on the John Newbery Medal and procedure for Newbery Book Club

Accelerated Reader (AR) quizzes (optional)

Plaque and stand from trophy store

Name plates and lettering for the plaque

Luncheon

READ poster and software

Three Ring notebook

Reading log sheet for each reader

Die-cut figures for bulletin board

Small stickers

Follett Newbery Medal poster

Paperback copies of Newbery and Newbery honor titles

Implementation for Newbery Book Club

Preparation

Meet with your principal, library committee, school steering committee, and PTA. Discuss the purpose and procedures of the Newbery Book Club. Explain that this program has been a successful reading promotional program initiated by Ms. Linda Ward, Montclair Elementary School in Omaha, Nebraska, and is in place in many elementary and middle schools across the country. Discussing the program can result in financial support. Teachers may be willing to shift some grade-level funding for books and quizzes. The principal may find some school partners or community members to help with the cost of the plaque, name plates, and luncheon. The PTA may assist with the funding for Newbery Book Club. The trophy store and local printer also may provide some discounts on the plaque, name plates, lettering, and posters.

At the beginning of the school year, present a slideshow and discuss the John Newbery Medal and Newbery Book Club with fourth through eighth graders. Invite everyone to participate by reading 10 Newbery Award and Honor books during the school year. Books can be read, listened to on audiobooks, or read to the child by a teacher or parent. After the book is completed, students take an AR quiz or complete a story map. Record a book as completed with

Celebrating a reading achievement with family.

A proud moment with the Newbery plaque.

an 80-percent or above AR quiz score or an acceptable story map. Story maps are read by the school librarian and child's language arts teacher. Students pass *Joyful Noise* by memorizing two of the poems of their choosing and reciting them for the principal, their teacher, or the librarian. One retake is allowed for a test not passed. Students record books read and test or story map score in the Newbery Club notebook. Each student has an individual page to record his reading. The librarian or library clerk initializes each book entered. The student then selects a die-cut figure, writes his name on it, and places a sticker on the figure for each completed book. Place the die-cut figure on the Newbery Award bulletin board. Reading for the Newbery Book Club begins during the first week of school and concludes two weeks prior to the end-of-the-school year.

When 10 books are successfully read, a brass name plate with the date a student has completed the reading is placed on the Newbery Book Club plaque. The plaque is on display in the foyer of the school for all to see. The principal personally congratulates the student in his classroom and makes a phone call to his family about this achievement. The student is also congratulated on the morning announcements. Students achieving this goal are invited to celebrate at a luncheon in the library with two family members. A READ poster with the student and his favorite Newbery book is created. The READ poster is presented to the student at the luncheon, along with a Newbery Award or Honor book and a picture of the student holding the Newbery plaque. A nice touch is to invite a community celebrity to be the guest speaker at the luncheon. This adds to the importance of the students' achievement.

Results

When surveyed about Newbery Book Club, students reported "it made me read ten books I would not have picked to read" or "I liked reading the different kinds of books that were longer and harder than the usual kinds of books I like."

Students encouraged one another to complete the reading, suggested various titles, and read together.

✦ The number of Newbery Award and Honor titles read increased dramatically. Twenty-six students read 10 or more Newbery titles in 1 year.

✦ A fourth-grade student read 25 Newbery titles in one school year.

✦ One student read all of the Newbery titles over several years.

✦ Students discovered and read series of books such as <u>The Moffats</u> after reading *Ginger Pye*; <u>The Shiloh Trilogy</u> and <u>The Dark Is Rising</u> series after reading *The Grey King*; and <u>The Giver</u> series.

✦ Students surveyed reported enjoying the "challenge" and being surprised at how "good" the books are.

✦ Parents surveyed reported enjoying observing their child work throughout the year on a goal, reading quality literature, and being recognized for an academic achievement.

✦ Students invited the owners of the trophy store and print shop to the luncheon to thank them for the donations of name plates and READ posters.

Step-by-Step Planning for Newbery Book Club

End of the School Year (May/June)

✦ Meet with committees and principal to discuss and go forward with the Newbery Book Club.

✦ Meet with the PTA at their final meeting to discuss the Newbery Book Club.

✦ Check collection and AR quizzes for Newbery titles and honor books.

✦ Order necessary book titles and quizzes.

✦ Meet with the public library youth librarians to explain the program and check the collection for available titles. Direct students to the public library for books too.

✦ Create slideshow for the Newbery Book Club presentation.

✦ Request Newbery posters from Follett. They will donate posters for the library and classrooms.

Beginning of the School Year (August/September)

✦ Introduce the Newbery Book Club to students.

✦ Set up a Newbery display area with the Follett poster, Newbery notebook, and Newbery titles.

◆ Set up Newbery Book Club bulletin board.

◆ Order the Newbery Book Club plaque.

Throughout the year

◆ Monitor and encourage student progress in the Newbery notebook.

◆ Book talk Newbery titles.

◆ Order name plates as students complete reading. Students may recertify.

◆ Make READ posters of students with their favorite Newbery titles.

◆ Celebrate the latest Newbery books in January. Order newest titles.

◆ Collect Newbery titles for end-of-the-year luncheon from Scholastic book fairs and book clubs for table decorations and student give-aways.

April

◆ Remind participating students of reading deadline.

◆ Secure date and funding for luncheon.

◆ Secure guest speaker for luncheon.

◆ Decide where luncheon will take place—library, classroom, or all-purpose room.

◆ Request adult volunteers to assist with luncheon.

May (two weeks prior to luncheon)

◆ Remind participating students of reading deadline.

◆ Send out Newbery Club luncheon invitation.

◆ Contact guest speaker to remind her of the engagement.

◆ Poll students and secure luncheon food with caterer. Pizza, breadsticks, sub sandwiches, chips, cookies, and sports drinks are well received.

One week prior to luncheon

◆ Continue to encourage students to complete the reading goal.

◆ Continue to order name plates and READ posters as students finish reading.

◆ Tally number of guests attending luncheon.

◆ Set aside school tablecloths or purchase disposable tablecloths.

◆ Have coolers available for drinks.

One or Two Days before Luncheon

✦ Send final number to caterer.

✦ Discuss luncheon etiquette with attendees. Students must meet guests at the door with a name tag and escort them to a table. Students should invite students without a guest to sit with them.

Dad and daughter enjoying Newbery Club Luncheon.

The Day of the Luncheon

The luncheon is on a tight schedule as students and guests have short lunch breaks.

✦ Set up area for luncheon.

✦ Have plaque(s) and READ posters on display.

✦ Students arrive 10 minutes earlier than guests.

✦ Review manners.

✦ Guests arrive, students greet.

✦ Food arrives at the same time as guests arrive.

✦ Set up food quickly and invite guests to lunch.

✦ Once everyone is seated and eating, librarian thanks guests for attending.

✦ Librarian explains the importance of goal and introduces guest speaker.

✦ Guest speaker speaks for 10 minutes.

✦ Librarian introduces each student to stand and be recognized for achievement. Plaque and READ posters are shown. Thank parents/caregivers for their encouragement.

A celebration luncheon.

- ✦ Adult volunteer photographs luncheon and students with Newbery plaque.
- ✦ Students are welcome to select a Newbery book and are dismissed.
- ✦ Clean up luncheon area.

STATE AWARD BOOK CLUB

PURPOSE

To encourage children to read annual State Award books.

To promote recreational reading.

GOALS

To promote reading of annual State Award books.

To encourage readers to vote for their favorite State Award book.

To build a recreational reading habit.

To increase vocabulary.

To improve comprehension and discussion skills.

To become part of a community of readers.

MATERIALS

- ✦ Multiple copies of State Award titles (many are in paperback)
- ✦ Book talks and book trailers
- ✦ Book display of State Award titles
- ✦ Attendance notebook
- ✦ Stopwatch
- ✦ Decorated question box
- ✦ State Award book kits from State Award book committee
- ✦ Light refreshments (small sizes of drinks, cheese sticks, crackers, grapes, and orange slices)
- ✦ Volunteer facilitators

Implementation

Many states have yearly book award lists. These lists are carefully compiled by librarians and teachers, and sometimes highlight local authors' titles. Read the guidelines your state has developed for reading and voting. Many State Award book committees provide book talks, trailers, and numerous activities using the selections. Guidelines explain when voting needs to be completed and supply the ballots. Generally, children must read a particular number of titles or hear them read aloud by a teacher in order to vote for a favorite title. Check with your public library for additional copies for children to check out as they promote the State Award books too.

There are several ways to promote the State Award books so that children will read them. Use an eye-catching display, a slideshow, book talks, and book trailers to entice readers. Providing a weekly book discussion is an additional way. A 30-minute session during the school day, at lunch or before school, gets kids talking about the State Award titles. This can be a drop-in activity or require a sign-up to plan for snacks and space. Publicize the book group during class visits and announcements. Use posters, school website, and a book display to get students' attention. Ask teachers to "talk it up" in class. Teachers, your principal, and public librarian can help you facilitate the discussion. Select a timekeeper and keep attendance logs. Each participant is allowed three minutes to describe the book she just completed or as far as she has read. Next use a "round robin" round using a question and answer from the question box. Each participant selects a question and has two to three minutes to answer. To wrap up the discussion, each person says the title of her favorite book thus far. Children then return the book they have completed and pick out new books for next week. Your public librarian may hold titles for kids if the title they want is checked out at school. Light refreshments can be served if desired but keep it simple. Participating students are recognized for attendance and number of books read in the State Book Award Club during the year-end awards assembly.

Round Robin Questions for the Question Box

+ Who was your favorite character? Why?
+ Was there a character that you did not care for? Why?
+ Describe the setting(s) of the book.
+ Does the title have a meaning? Explain.
+ Was there a mystery to solve? Describe.
+ Were the characters friends or not? Describe.
+ Did the book take place during an historical event? Explain.
+ Describe or read a funny part.

- ✦ Describe or read something scary.
- ✦ Describe or read something sad.
- ✦ Have you read other books by this author? What were they? How do they compare with this book?
- ✦ Describe a character's problem or quest.
- ✦ Did a character you like do something you didn't like? Explain.
- ✦ Was the end satisfying or not? Describe why or why not.

(Put the questions on slips of paper and laminate for repeated uses.)

Step-by-Step Planning for State Award Book Club

End of the School Year (May/June)

- ✦ Order copies of State Award titles.
- ✦ Discuss book group with teachers and principal. Invite them to facilitate with you.
- ✦ Read titles over the summer.
- ✦ Check State Book Award website for book talks, book marks, and activities.

Beginning of the School Year (August/September)

- ✦ Create a State Book Award display.
- ✦ Book talk several titles with students.
- ✦ Use slideshow to explain State Book Award discussion group.

Weekly until Voting Occurs

- ✦ Continue to book talk the books.
- ✦ Meet and discuss books.
- ✦ Enjoy snacks.
- ✦ Keep a list of which book students pick as their favorite each week.

Voting

- ✦ Involve students who have read required titles to vote for their favorite.
- ✦ Send results to State Award Book committee.
- ✦ Announce State Award winner.
- ✦ Recognize readers at end-of-the-year school assembly with a certificate.

(Your School) Newbery Book Club Log

Name_____Grade____Homeroom_____

Date	Title	Test Score	Story Map Score	Read Independently (I) or Read to (T)	Verification

 From *For the Love of Reading: Guide to K–8 Reading Promotions* by Nancy L. Baumann. Santa Barbara, CA: Libraries Unlimited. Copyright © 2013.

Newbery Club Luncheon

You and two adults from your family are invited to attend the Newbery Club Luncheon.

When: (Insert date)

Time: (Insert time)

Where: (Insert place)

Please <u>RSVP</u> to (your name) if you will be attending the luncheon and the number of guests.

• •

I, (student name)_____, will attend the luncheon.

The number of guests attending is 1 or 2 (circle number).

Return this form to (your name) by (date).

 **Notes**

Appendix I:
Vendors, Journals, and Further Reading

Beary Special Readers

Badge-A-Minit
345 North Lewis Ave.
Oglesby, IL 61348
Phone: 800.223.4103
Fax: 815.883.9696
www.badgeaminit.com

Early Bird Readers

Bearport Publishing Company, Inc.
45 West 21st Street, Suite B
New York, NY 10010
Phone: 877.337.8577
Fax: 866.337.8557
www.bearportpublishing.com

Capstone Publishing
P.O. Box No. 669
Mankato, MN 56002-0669
Phone: 800.747.4992
Fax: 888.262.0705
www.capstonepub.com

Scholastic Inc.
557 Broadway
New York, NY 10012
Phone: 800.724.6527 Press 2
www.scholastic.com

Oriental Trading Company
4206 South 108th Street
Omaha, NE 68137
Phone: 800.875.8480
Fax: 800.327.8904
www.orientaltrading.com

Raymond Geddes
7110 Belair Rd., Suite 200
Baltimore, MD 21206
Phone: 888.431.1722
Fax: 800.533.3359
www.raymondgeddes.com

Dollar General
100 Mission Rdg
Goodlettsville TN 37072
Phone: 615.855.4000
Fax: 615.855.5252
www.dollargeneral.com

American Library Association
(ALA)
READ Design Studio Products
50 East Huron Street
Chicago, Illinois 60611-2795
Phone: 312.944.6780
Fax: 312.440.9374
www.alastore.ala.org

Mock Newbery Book Club

Mock Newbery and Caldecott Mock Elections Tool Kit—www.alastore.ala.org

Journals and Publications

School Library Journal—slj.com

Horn Book—www.hbook.com

School Library Monthly—www.schoolmonthly.com

Library Media Connection—www.librarymediaconnection.com

Knowledge Quest/American Association of School Librarians (AASL)—www.knowledgequest.com

Library Sparks—www.librarysparks.com

The Reading Teacher, Journal of Adolescent & Adult Literacy, Reading Research Quarterly (peer reviewed journals of The International Reading Association)—www.reading.org

Appendix II: Websites

Cooperative Children's Book Center—http://www.education.wisc.edu/ccbc/

Association for Library Service to Children (ALSC)—http://www.ala.org/alsc/compubs/booklists

Children's Choices & Young Adult Choices, International Reading Association (IRA)—http://www.reading.org/Resources/Booklists/ChildrensChoices.aspx and http://www.reading.org/resources/booklists/youngadultschoices.aspx

School Library Journal Best Books List—http://www.slj.com/2012/11/featured/best-books-2012/

Boston Globe–Horn Book Award List—http://www.hbook.com/2012/06/news/boston-globe-horn-book-awards/2012-boston-globe-horn-book-awards-for-excellence-in-childrens-literature/

Read Kiddo Read—http://www.readkiddoread.com/home

School Library Journal Heavy Medal Blog—http://blogs.slj.com/heavymedal/

School Library Journal Good Comics for Kids Blog—http://blogs.slj.com/goodcomicsforkids/

Beyond the Book Storytimes Blog—http://btbstorytimes.blogspot.com/

YA Books, Book Trailers, and More—http://www.naomibates.blogspot.com/ and http://booktrailersforallsearch.com/

readingrockets.org

adlit.org

Appendix III:
Sample Booktalks for Reading Lunch

The Million Dollar Shot

by Dan Gutman

When Eddie Ball discovers that he has won a poetry contest, he is so excited. His prize is a chance to win 1 million dollars. He could win 1 million dollars by sinking a free throw at the NBA finals. Boy oh boy, would that be terrific. Eddie's dad died and his mom is struggling with a low paying job at the Finkle Foods Factory to support them. If you are wondering what a Finkle is, it is something like a Hostess Twinkie. It is a dessert cake made of caramel, peanuts, and marshmallow, rolled in dough, deep fried, and then covered in Chocolate!!! Yum!!! A Finkle was named after George Finkle, the person who invented them. Eddie is determined to win the million dollars, but he is going to have to improve his shooting because he only will get one shot, one chance. His friend, Annie, is a terrific shot. She can even make free throws with her eyes closed. Annie tries to help Eddie but he brushes her off. The next day, Annie's father, Mr. Stokely, comes over to help Eddie learn how to shoot free throws so he can win the million dollar prize. Mr. Stokely was an outstanding college player and almost became a pro player but blew his chance because he goofed off, stopped going to class and got real lazy. When his tryouts came for the Lakers, they didn't even draft him. So he ended up working at the Finkle Food Factory. Mr. Stokely has a special method for shooting foul shots that teaches Eddie how to shoot almost 90 percent of his shots from the line! Eddie is now feeling like he COULD win the million dollar prize. Then one day, Eddie and Annie came home from school, and find their parents home from work early. They had been laid off from their jobs at the Finkle Food Factory. Mr. Finkle's factory is in financial trouble so he is laying workers off. Eddie realizes he really needs to win the million dollars for his mom and if he wins, he'll share with Annie and her dad. But Mr. Finkle himself shows up at Eddie's house and offers to give his mom her job back and a paid college education if Eddie will miss the free throw on PURPOSE! He says his company will be in big financial trouble if Eddie wins the contest. Mr. Finkle tells Eddie he must keep this a secret. Eddie doesn't know what to do—if he misses on purpose, his mom will get her job back, and college will be paid for; if he goes for it, he could win the money; and if he goes for it and misses, he will get nothing. What should he do? To find out, come and listen to **The Million Dollar Shot**.

Kensuke's Kingdom

by Michael Morpurgo

Eleven-year-old Michael, his dog Stella, and his family were happy and living a good life until his father and mother were laid off from their jobs. His family lost everything. The next thing Michael knew was that his father sold the family car and bought a 42-foot sailboat called the "Peggy Sue." His father wanted them to sail around the world. At first, Michael and his mother thought his dad was crazy. But Michael's dad insisted and was excited about sailing to places they had only read about in books. He convinced Michael's mom to take sailing and navigating lessons from Barnacle Bill, an experienced sailor. Finally, Bill was satisfied with their sailing progress. The entire family including Stella set sail for their around the world adventure. Michael's best friend, Eddie, came to say good bye and gave Michael a soccer ball. Little did Michael realize that the soccer ball would save his life. One night Michael and Stella fell overboard when the "Peggy Sue" suddenly veered sideways. Michael was not wearing his life jacket! And what about Stella? Michael yelled and screamed but his parents were sleeping in the cabin and couldn't hear him. He watched as the "Peggy Sue" sailed farther and farther away. Can Michael and Stella survive in shark-infested waters? Can he save himself and Stella? To find out, come and listen to **Kensuke's Kingdom**.

Ruby Holler

by Sharon Creech

Dallas and Florida are nicknamed "The Trouble Twins." It is not their fault either. The people who want to adopt them don't understand them. Neither do the Trepids who run the orphanage where Dallas and Florida live. The problem is that everyone has too many rules. Dallas and Florida can't help it if they like to run or talk or yell.

The twins have been shuffled between many foster families and orphanages all the 13 years of their lives. They would love to find a place to call home but creepy and mean Mr. and Mrs. Trepid, who run the orphanage, keep giving Dallas and Florida to people who are mean or end up not really liking children. Dallas and Florida keep getting returned to the orphanage until one day an older couple named Tiller and Sairy show up and take Dallas and Florida home with them to a place called Ruby Holler. Tiller and Sairy's children are all grown up and they want to take one last adventure trip while their bodies can still paddle canoes and climb mountains. They want Dallas and Florida to accompany them on their adventures. At first, Dallas and Florida are very suspicious. No one has ever been this kind to them at any other foster home. Oh no!!! At the other foster homes, people have hit them and locked them in damp dark basements with lizards and rats. And no one has ever fed them as good of food as Sairy cooks. Florida thinks Sairy and Tiller are trying to fatten them up, like Hansel and Gretel, and will try to stick them in the oven. Florida warns Dallas not to eat too much!! To find out what happens to Dallas and Florida in their new foster home, come and listen to **Ruby Holler**.

Mrs. Frisby and the Rats of NIMH

by Robert C. O'Brien

When Mrs. Frisby's youngest child Timothy becomes gravely ill, she seeks help from Mr. Ages, an elderly white mouse, who has given her medicine for Timothy in the past. Mrs. Frisby is a widow and is very upset because she overheard Farmer Fitzgibbon declare he was going to begin spring plowing soon. This means Mrs. Frisby and her family will have to move immediately. The cinderblock where she and her children live is located in the field that Farmer Fitzgibbon would be plowing soon. But Mr. Ages advises not to move Timothy for at least a month because of his pneumonia. Mrs. Frisby is understandably upset. Mr. Ages recommends that she ask the wise old owl to suggest a solution to her problem. When the owl discovers that Mrs. Frisby was Jonathan Frisby's widow, he is VERY eager to help her. The owl sends Mrs. Frisby to see the rats living under the rosebush. The owl felt that rats could move Mrs. Frisby's house to a safer place, away from the plow.

While Mrs. Frisby is confused about the rats' providing assistance, the owl insists she go and meet with Nicodemus and Justin, the rats in charge of the colony. After Mrs. Frisby gains entrance to the rats' home, she is astounded beyond belief. The rats are extremely sophisticated, they can read, have their home wired for electricity, and have many inventions known only to people. They also never AGE, or grow older. The rats, favorably impressed with her being Jonathan Frisby's widow, agree to help Mrs. Frisby move her cinderblock home and save her family from the farmer's plow. But how, she wonders, did the rats learn to read, use electricity, and why do they never get older??? How did they become so intelligent and civilized? Mrs. Frisby knows that the rats can explain what happened to her husband, Jonathan. All she knew was one day he never came home. To discover the mystery of how the rats became so intelligent and if Mrs. Frisby teams up with the rats to save her family, come and listen to **Mrs. Frisby and the Rats of NIMH**.

Crash

by Jerry Spinelli

Crash, alias John Coogan, got his name from crashing into his little cousin Bridget and knocking her clear out of the house. Crash is a big-time JOCK and proud of it. He is pushy, obnoxious, and thinks he is God's gift to the young ladies. Football means everything to Crash. His best friend in the seventh grade is Mike DeLuca. Mike dares Crash to play mean practical jokes on lots of kids at school. Mike helps Crash play these jokes on unsuspecting kids; they are bullies. Their favorite target is Penn Webb—the nerdiest, dweebiest kid around. Pretty soon, what goes around comes around. Crash must decide who his "real friends" are. To find out how bullying can get out of hand, and how Crash, the football hero, must decide which side he is really on, come and listen to **Crash** by Jerry Spinelli.

The Ghost of Fossil Glen

by Cynthia DeFelice

Allie Nichols clung to the side of the steep cliff, hanging on for dear life. "How stupid can I be," she asked herself. Her parents had warned her over and over not to go fossil hunting alone in Fossil Glen, that it was dangerous. But Allie knew the best fossils were up in the cliffs. "Oh well," thought Allie, "at least Mom and Dad won't have to kill me, I will already be dead from falling 100 feet straight down." Suddenly, Allie heard a voice, not a voice she recognized but it seemed kind of familiar. It was soft and soothing and seemed to be coming from inside of her head. She trusted it right away. "Go ahead, said the voice. It will be all right. Go, slide down the tree root, do it before you get so tired you simply fall." Allie followed the voice's direction, and continued as the voice told her to "slide, don't lean back, just let yourself slide." Allie slid all the way down the side of the cliff. She was scratched, bruised, bloody, and dirty but she was alive and had a great trilobite, a fossil, the best one ever for her collection. But that afternoon Allie continued to wonder about the mysterious voice. She called her friend, Dub to tell him about her adventure. Dub was impressed but reminded Allie that she needed to be careful. Then Dub reminded Allie about needing a journal for school as part of language arts assignment. Allie had forgotten to get a notebook. She knew her mother would be unhappy about having to go out and get her one. As Allie was sorting through the mail while discussing the journal with Dub, she came upon a wrapped package with her name on it. Nothing else—no address, last name or stamp, just *Allie* written on the outside. She opened the package and found a beautiful red leather book with blank pages. Allie got the same funny feeling she felt when she heard the mysterious voice. A chill ran down her spine. Allie hung up from Dub, and closed her eyes, and held the book tightly to her. As before, a chill settled over her, raising the flesh on her arms and the little hairs on the back of her neck. Her eyes were still closed when a face appeared in her mind's eye. It was a girl about her own age, with curly black hair floating around her face in a cloud and her dark eyes penetrated Allie's. Her arms reached toward Allie, and the girl's lips moved, calling to Allie. "Help me, help me!" Allie had never seen this girl before. The next day, Allie remembered she had to write an entry in her red book for school. She went to get the book in her room. She had left it on her desk. But when she got into her room, she stopped! Her heart lurched! The book was open but she had left it closed. The air in her bedroom felt very chilly. Allie looked at her journal. On the first page, she saw writing—I am L and the L trailed off as if the writer had been interrupted suddenly. She remembered looking through every page when she was talking to Dub. The journal was blank. Who is L? Why is Allie hearing voices? Is L the ghost of a girl who went missing from Fossil Glen four years ago? Come and listen to ***The Ghost of Fossil Glen*** if you like ghost stories and mysteries.

Gregor the Overlander

by Suzanne Collins

Eleven-year-old Gregor is really frustrated. Here it is—the first day of summer vacation and what is he doing? Babysitting his grandmother and his two-year-old sister Boots. His grandmother doesn't even know who he is half the time and calls him Simon. "Who's Simon," wonders Gregor. Oh well, he has to try and make the best of it. He wants to help his mother. She had to go back to work after Gregor's father mysteriously disappeared two years ago. He heard whispers from kids at school and around his apartment building in New York City that his father deserted them. "My dad wouldn't do that to us," thought Gregor. He loved us, and he loved our family. He loved his job as a science teacher. Gregor heard a knock at the door. It was his neighbor, Mrs. Cormaci, who offered to sit with his grandmother while Gregor did the laundry in the basement of the apartment. Gregor offered Mrs. Cormaci a root beer and left with all the laundry. Walking slowly down the stairs to the basement, Gregor noticed that Boots was with him. Soon Gregor was sorting laundry and washing clothes while Boots chased an old tennis ball. Suddenly, Gregor heard Boots giggling. He hurried across the laundry room just in time to see Boots looking into a metal grate. Some steam or vapor was drifting out of the open grate and was curling around Boots. Boots held out her arms and leaned forward. "No," yelled Gregor. He lunged to try and grab Boots who seemed to be sucked down into the air duct. Gregor shoved his head and shoulders into the 2 × 2-foot hole. The metal grate clunked him on his back and the next thing he knew he was falling! Gregor twisted around in the air and tried to grab onto something but he only came up empty. "Boots, Boots," he hollered. "Ge-go, I go wheeeee," said Boots. She thinks she is on a big slide. At least, she is not afraid thought Gregor. Gregor fell and fell, was he in a dream?? The mist finally cleared, and Gregor heard a small thump and the patter of little sandals. "Ahh," Boots landed. A few seconds later, Gregor's sneakers made contact with the ground. He was in total darkness. He heard Boots squeal, "Beeg Bug, Gee-go, Beeg Bug." Gregor rushed toward the small spot of light, squeezing himself through a narrow crevice. His sneaker caught on something, and Gregor tripped, landing on his hands and feet. When he looked up, he saw the biggest cockroach he had ever seen in his whole life! "Beeg Bug," squealed Boots.

Gregor found himself in Underland. It is a world under our world, inhabited by humans with purple eyes and thin white skin, giant cockroaches, spiders, and bats. But the scariest of all are giant rats who want to kill the humans and other animals and rule Underland. Gregor discovers the Underlanders have been waiting for him as has been revealed in a strange prophecy. Not only that, the people with the purple eyes tell Gregor that his father is in Underland and is being held as a prisoner by the rats. Gregor is reluctant to begin the quest to save the Underland. But he must save his father! How can he do this and take care of Boots. To find out, come and listen to **Gregor the Overlander**.

Travel Team

by Mike Lupica

Imagine you have played basketball on the same travel team since fifth grade. Then at tryouts, you get cut! You get cut because you have barely grown since fifth grade. You are a great ball handler and accurately pass the ball. You are one of the quickest guys on the team. But you are cut because the coaches are going for height this year in order to win the championship.

This is what happened to Danny Walker. He is devastated and angry too. His mom feels bad for Danny and explains what happened to Danny's father, Richie Walker, a former NBA star. Richie's career was cut short by an automobile injury. Danny's parents split up after the accident. Now Richie Walker is back in town and working to get his life back together. He knows Danny shouldn't have been cut. He is too good of a player. After all who taught him the game!!

Imagine Danny's surprise when his Dad offers to coach a newly formed team for Danny. There aren't many players to choose from at this late date but Danny and his dad put together a team. Danny and the "Rugrats" (aka "Warriors") were finishing up practice when his dad spotted an extraordinary player warming up in the gym. Colby Danes, playing with the seventh grade girls' travel team, has all the right moves. The next thing Danny knows, Colby is playing with them, the Warriors.

The season begins, and the Warriors lose every game. Danny is discouraged but his dad isn't. Richie can see that the Warriors are losing by less each time they play, gaining skills and confidence and finally they win one by 20 points. The team goes crazy. They finally believe they can be contenders in each game. Everyone is going to Fierro's Pizza to celebrate. Danny goes there with his mom. They'll meet his dad there too. But his dad didn't show. His mom believes his dad is back to his old ways of having too much to drink after a game. But then they get a phone call. There has been an accident, a bad accident.

Danny's dad has a broken hip and shoulder, and a collapsed lung. His dad lost control of his car. But he didn't break his promise of not drinking anymore. He was sober.

But now who will coach the team, now that they are finally able to play competitively? Will the team have to forfeit the rest of the season? You will be amazed at who steps in and takes charge of the team and brings them to the finals of the tournament. To find out, come and listen to **Travel Team** by Mike Lupica.

The One and Only Ivan

by K. A. Applegate

Ivan is a handsome silverback gorilla. He exists at the Exit 8 Big Top Mall and Video Arcade along with Stella, an elderly elephant, and some monkeys and parrots. Ivan's life has been reduced to having people watch him through the glass, watch old television shows, and make me-balls to throw at humans. Me-balls are made by rolling up dung into the size of a small apple and letting them dry. Ivan does have more friends besides Stella. Bob, a stray dog, Julia and her father, George, also are friends of Ivan. George cleans at the mall, and Julia comes along. George insists Julia work on her homework while he is cleaning, but Julia likes to draw. Ivan also likes to draw things he has seen, such as a beetle or a banana. Sometimes, he thinks of what his life was like before he was captured along with his twin sister.

One day, Ivan learns that a new member is going to join Stella and him at the Exit 8 Big Top Mall and Video Arcade. A baby elephant, named Ruby, arrives to increase business. Poor Ruby, she is terrified, sad, and lonely. Stella, the old elephant, comforts Ruby and tries to answer her questions. All the residents of Exit 8 Big Top Mall know what Ruby's life is going to be like, and they are saddened beyond belief. Mack, the owner of the mall and the animals, is only interested in money and not the animals' well-being. After Stella dies from Mack's negligence, Ivan, Bob, and Julia each decide they are going to help Ruby find a new life, a life at a zoo where she will be cared for and protected. But how? How can Ivan, a captive in a glass cage; Bob, a stray dog; and Julia, a child, convince humans that Ruby must get to a zoo. To find out, come to Reading Lunch and listen to **The One and Only Ivan** by K. A. Applegate. This book is based on a true story of a gorilla that lived in a shopping mall in Washington state.

Three Times Lucky

by Sheila Turnage

Moses "Mo" LoBeau has a mysterious life. Eleven years ago, she was discovered floating on a raft downstream after a fierce hurricane blew through the tiny town of Tupelo Landing, North Carolina. Baby Mo was rescued from the rushing water by the Colonel. However, the Colonel is suffering from amnesia and has no memory of who he was or why he was at the creek when the hurricane struck. The Colonel and his partner, Miss Lana, now own and operate the only café in town. Mysteries seem to follow Mo. Who was her mother and how did they become separated? Who is the Colonel and why did he develop amnesia? Determined to find out, Mo puts messages in bottles and drops them in the creek for someone to help her find her "Upstream Mother." But searching for her mother is interrupted when local curmudgeon and tightwad Mr. Jesse is found murdered. Mo's best friend Dale Earnhardt Johnson III is a suspect since he stole Mr. Jesse's boat. Now Mo must use her detective skills to prove Dale is innocent, but also discover who the murderer is before someone else dies. To find out who murdered Mr. Jesse, who is the Colonel, and where is Mo's mother, come to Reading Lunch and listen to **Three Times Lucky** by Sheila Turnage.

The False Prince

by Jennifer Nielsen

Prince Jaron mysteriously drowned in an accident at sea! Or did he? With the rest of the royal family murdered, and civil war on the horizon, Conner, a nobleman, devises a plot to pass off an orphan as Prince Jaron. Then Conner can control the fake prince and the kingdom from behind the scenes. Conner and his henchmen scour the streets for orphans and runaways who resemble Prince Jaron. Once he has found four boys that will work, he transports them to his manor to school them into becoming Prince Jaron. All the boys except one, Sage, are excited to be rescued from their former lives. Having food, shelter, and comforts outweigh being Conner's puppet. Sage is not so sure he wants to participate in Conner's scheme. To intimidate the boys, Conner orders one of them, the weakest, to be shot with an arrow in the chest in front of them. This subdues any thoughts of resistance from the orphans. At the manor, the boys are pitted against one another since only one imposter can be selected. The rest will die since Conner can't take a chance of them telling anyone about the plot. Who will be the best at sword fighting, equestrian skills, dancing, and royal etiquette? Sage is the best choice but will his attitude and mouthiness lead to his death? Will Conner's plan succeed? What will happen to the rejected orphans? To find out, come to Reading Lunch and listen to **The False Prince** by Jennifer Nielsen.

A View from the Cherry Tree

by Willo Davis Roberts

Rob's sister is getting married, and his whole life is messed up because of the dumb wedding. Getting bored with the whole wedding thing, Rob went and sat in the cherry tree. The cherry tree is between his house and his neighbor's, Mrs. Calloway. From his perch in the cherry tree, Rob can see right into Mrs. Calloway's house. She was really mean, and she was always complaining about Rob's cat. When Rob was little, he thought Mrs. Calloway caught kids and put them in her oven. Then she ate them like the witch in Hansel and Gretel. Now that he was older, he doesn't believe that anymore, but he'd never go inside her house for anything. One day when the wedding plans got way too crazy for Rob, he made himself some sandwiches, stuffed his pockets with cookies, grabbed a Pepsi from the fridge, and went to sit up in the cherry tree. That was how he happened to see the murder of Mrs. Calloway. He saw someone push her—great big hands that pushed her out of the window. She got caught by her binocular strap on the branch of the cherry tree, and Rob watched her hang there and die! Rob told his parents that Mrs. Calloway was dead. Not only was she dead, she was murdered. His parents won't listen to him and neither do the police officers. Rob gives up. He is starting to believe he has an overactive imagination like everyone is telling him, but then strange things begin to happen to Rob. A heavy pot falls and almost hits Rob on the head. Then he discovers his dinner turns out to be laced with POISON. Rob knows that Mrs. Calloway was murdered and he is terrified that he will be the next victim! To find out who murdered Mrs. Calloway and is trying to murder Rob, come and listen to **A View From the Cherry Tree** by Willo Davis Roberts.

Appendix IV: Common Core State Standards/ AASL Standards for 21st-Century Learners and Reading Promotional Programs Chart

Reading Program	Phonological Awareness	Print Concepts	Vocabulary Acquisition and Use	Phonics and Word Recognition	Read Emergent Text	Key Ideas and Details
Beary Special Readers	X	X	X	X	X	X
Early Bird Readers			X	X		X
Reading Lunch			X			X
Mock Newbery Book Group			X	X		X
State Award Book Reading Group			X	X		X
Newbery Book Club			X	X		X
One Book One School			X	X		X
Battle of the Books			X	X		X
Reading Millionaires	X	X	X	X	X	X

For a detailed look at the standards, see http://www.ala.org/aasl/guidelinesandstandards/commoncorecrosswalk/English.

Craft and Structure	Fluency	Integration of Knowledge, Ideas, and Structure	Range of Reading Complexity of Text	Research to Build and Present Knowledge	Comprehension and Collaboration	Text Types and Purposes
X	X	X		X	X	
X	X	X	X	X	X	
X		X		X	X	
X	X	X	X	X	X	X
X	X	X	X	X	X	X
X	X	X	X	X	X	X
X	X	X	X	X	X	
X		X	X	X	X	
X	X	X	X	X	X	

Works Cited

"AASL Standards for the 21st-Century Learner: American Association
of School Librarians (AASL)." *American Library Association.*
http://www.ala.org/aasl/guidelinesandstandards/learningstandards/
standards (accessed September 2, 2012).

Allington, Richard L. *What Really Matters for Struggling Readers: Design-
ing Research-based Programs.* 3rd ed. Boston: Pearson, 2012.

Anderson, Richard C. *Becoming a Nation of Readers: The Report of the
Commission on Reading.* Washington, DC: National Academy of
Education, 1985.

Biancarosa, C., and C.E. Snow. "Reading Next: A Vision for Action and
Research in Middle and High School Literacy (Second edition)—
Reading & Writing—Resource Collections—Literacy Information
and Communication System (LINCS)." The Literacy Information and Communication System (LINCS). http://lincs.ed.gov/
lincs/resourcecollections/readingandwriting/profile_17 (accessed
September 3, 2012).

Blessing, Candy. "Reading to Kids who Are Old Enough to Shave." *School
Library Journal*, April 1, 2005. http://www.schoollibraryjournal
.com/article/CA514023.html (accessed September 2, 2012).

Cunningham, Anne, and Keith Stanovich. "Reading Can Make You
Smarter." *Principal* 83, no. 2 (November/December 2003): 34–39.

"Family-School Partnerships: Essential Elements of Literacy Instruction in
the United States." *International Reading Association*, 2000. http://
www.reading.org/Libraries/position-statements-and-resolutions/
ps1053_family.pdf (accessed September 2, 2012).

Fox, Mem. *Reading Magic: Why Reading Aloud to Our Children Will
Change Their Lives Forever*, updated and revised ed. New York: Harcourt, 2008.

Gallagher, Kelly. *Readicide: How Schools Are Killing Reading and What
You Can Do About It.* Portland, ME: Stenhouse Publishers, 2009.

Gambrell, Linda. "Seven Rules of Engagement: What's Most Important to Know About Motivation to Read." *The Reading Teacher* 65, no. 3 (2011): 172–78.

Garan, Elaine, and Glenn DeVoogd. "The Benefits of Sustained Silent Reading: Scientific Research and Common Sense Converge." *The Reading Teacher* 62, no. 4 (2008): 336–44.

Hall, Susan L., and Louisa C. Moats. "Why Reading to Children Is Important." *American Educator* 24, no. 1 (Spring 2000): 26–33.

Hernandez, Donald. "Education—Double Jeopardy: How Third-Grade Reading Skills and Poverty Influence High School Graduation." *The Annie E. Casey Foundation*, 2012. http://www.aecf.org/KnowledgeCenter/Education.aspx (accessed September 2, 2012).

Ivey, Gay, and Karen Broaddus. " 'Just Plain Reading' ": A Survey of What Makes Students Want to Read in Middle School Classrooms." *Reading Research Quarterly* 36, no. 4 (2001): 350–77.

Krashen, Stephen D. *The Power of Reading: Insights from the Research.* 2nd ed. Westport, CT: Libraries Unlimited, 2004.

Krashen, Stephen. "Free Reading." *Library Journal*, September 1, 2006. http://www.libraryjournal.com/article/CA6367048.html (accessed September 2, 2012).

Kozol, Jonathan. "The Other America." *School Library Journal* (August 2012): 25–27.

Lautenschlager, John, and Karl Hertz. "Inexpensive, Worthwhile, Educational: Parents Reading to Children." *The Reading Teacher* 38, no. 1 (1984): 18–20.

Lee, Valarie. "Becoming the Reading Mentors Our Adolescents Deserve: Developing a Successful Sustained Silent Reading Program." *Journal of Adolescent & Adult Literacy* 55, no. 3 (2011): 209–18.

Moss, Barbara, and Terrell A. Young. *Creating Lifelong Readers through Independent Reading.* Newark, DE: International Reading Association, 2010.

Neuman, Susan B. *Literacy in the Television Age: The Myth of the TV Effect.* 2nd ed. Norwood, NJ: Ablex, 1995.

Neuman, Susan B., and Donna Celano. "Access to Print in Low-Income and Middle-Income Communities: An Ecological Study of Four Neighborhoods." *Reading Research Quarterly* 36, no. 1 (2001): 8–26.

Pilgreen, Janice L. *The SSR Handbook: How to Organize and Manage a Sustained Silent Reading Program.* Portsmouth, NH: Boynton/Cook Publishers, 2000.

Preddy, Leslie. *Social Readers: Promoting Reading in the 21st Century.* Santa Barbara, CA: Libraries Unlimited, 2010.

Reutzel, D. Ray, Parker Fawson, and John Smith. "Reconsidering Silent Sustained Reading: An Exploratory Study of Scaffolded Silent Reading." *Journal of Educational Research* 102, no. 1 (2008): 37–50.

Sherman, Louise. "Have a Story Lunch." *School Library Journal* 33, no. 2 (October 1986): 120, 121.

Trelease, Jim. *The Read-Aloud Handbook.* 6th ed. New York: Penguin Books, 2006.

Worthy, Jo. "What Makes Intermediate-grade Students Want to Read?" *The Reading Teacher* 55, no. 6 (2002): 568, 569.

Zambo, Debby, and William G. Brozo. *Bright Beginnings for Boys: Engaging Young Boys in Active Literacy.* Newark, DE: International Reading Association, 2009.

Further Reading

Allington, Richard. "If They Don't Read Much, How They Ever Gonna Get Good?" *Journal of Reading* 21, no. 1 (1977): 57–61.

Applegate, Anthony, and Mary DeKonty. "A Study of Thoughtful Literacy and the Motivation to Read." *The Reading Teacher* 64, no. 4 (2010): 226–34.

Celano, Donna, and Susan Neuman. "When Schools Close, the Knowledge Gap Grows." *Phi Delta Kappan* 90, no. 4 (December 2008): 256–62.

"Crosswalk of the Common Core Standards and the Standards for the 21st-Century Learner: American Association of School Librarians (AASL)." *American Library Association.* http://www.ala.org/aasl/guideli nesandstandards/commoncorecrosswalk (accessed September 2, 2012).

Harvey, Carl A. *The 21st Century Elementary Library Media Program.* Santa Barbara, CA: Linworth Pub., 2010.

Hiebert, Elfrieda H., and D. Ray Reutzel. *Revisiting Silent Reading: New Directions for Teachers and Researchers.* Newark, DE: International Reading Association, 2010.

McGhee, Marla W., and Barbara A. Jansen. *The Principal's Guide to a Powerful Library Media Program a School Library for the 21st Century.* 2nd ed. Santa Barbara, CA: Linworth Pub., 2010.

Morgan, Denise, Maryann Mraz, Nancy Padak, and Timothy Rasinski. *Independent Reading.* New York: Guilford Press, 2009.

Morris, Betty J. *Administering the School Library Media Program.* 5th ed. Santa Barbara, CA: Libraries Unlimited, 2010.

Neuman, Susan, and Donna C. Celano. *Giving Our Children a Fighting Chance: Poverty, Literacy, and the Development of Information Capital.* New York: Teachers College Press, 2012.

Pressley, Michael. *Motivating Primary-grade Students.* New York: Guilford Press, 2003.

Sadoski, Mark. "An Attitude Survey for Sustained Silent Reading Programs." *Journal of Reading* 23, no. 8 (1980): 721–26.

Shin, Fay H., and Stephen D. Krashen. *Summer Reading: Program and Evidence.* Boston: Pearson/Allyn and Bacon, 2008.

Stevens, Angela. " Poor Reading Skills Lead More Students to Dropout of
    School Than Poverty." *Reading Program: Reading Horizons*, April 20,
    2011. http://www.readinghorizons.com/blog/post/2011/04/20/.
Tucker, Cynthia. "Reading Rocks: It's Not too Late to Get in Step." *Atlanta
    Journal Constitution*, June 11, 2006, sec. Opinion.
Young, Terry. *School Libraries Work!*, updated AASL Conference ed. Danbury,
    CT: Scholastic Library Pub., 2008.

Index

Vendors, 89–90, 105

Volunteers: Beary Special Readers, 4–5, 11, 16; One Book One School Community Read, 82; Reading Millionaires Project, 111

Websites: Battle of the Books, 105; One Book One School Community Read, 89–91; Reading Millionaires Project, 116

About the Author

NANCY L. BAUMANN, MLS, is instructor at the University of Missouri School of Information Science and Learning Technology, Columbia. She holds a master's degree in library science from the University of North Texas, Denton.